Table of Contents

DEDICATION

"This publication is respectfully dedicated to my ancestors who had the foresight and trust in God to bring their families, and thereby future generations, to Canada a land of freedom and promise. *Soli Deo Gloria.*"

ONE

Mennonite Roots

My name is John Edwin Warkentin. I was born August 1, 1923, to Dutch Mennonite immigrants on a farm at Haskett, Manitoba. My great-grandparents on my father's side settled in Kronsfeld, Manitoba, one of a number of Mennonite villages established in the 1870s. Haskett was started in 1907 by American entrepreneur John Haskett, who saw a financial opportunity, buying the property from Mr. Bernhard Krahn. Haskett had a school, post office, general stores, grain elevators, lumberyards, farm machinery sales, and other farm-related enterprises. The closing of the railway (Great Northern Railway from Walhalla, North Dakota to Morden, Manitoba) in 1936 started a gradual decline of the business sector, and by 1971 the school closed after all the other businesses had closed. The first wave of emigrants from South Russia arrived in Canada on the SS Polynesian in the mid-1870s. Among the passenger list was a family led by Jacob and Helena Warkentin and their family of four sons and five daughters.

My great-grandfather, whom we'll call Jacob the Patriarch, was born 1822 and died 1919. He was married to Helena, who was born 1820 and died 1912. Their children were Peter, John, Helena,

Jacob, Cornelius, Maria, Sarah, Aganeta, and Isaac, who was born in Canada. Their son Jacob—my grandfather—later took J as a middle initial to help avoid confusion. You'll soon see why.

My grandfather Jacob J. Warkentin was born 1864 and died 1945. He too was married to a woman by the name of Helena. Helena Warkentin (née Brown) was born 1872 and died 1966. Their children were Jacob†, Helena†, Jacob, Mary, Katharine, Helen, Sarah, John, Anne, Susanna & Peter [twins], and Alice†. Their first two children as well as their last child died in infancy. Their second son named Jacob—my father—later took B as his middle initial for reasons similar to *his* father.

My father, Jacob B. Warkentin and his wife, Maria Düek (born 1897 and died 1991), were married in 1918. Their children were Jacob (Jack), John†, Cornelius Henry (Conn), John Edwin, Peter Earl, Doris Maureen, and Reginald George.

My mother's side of the family looks like this. My great-grandparents Peter Klassen and his wife Maria Klassen (née Redekopp) had a daughter Margaretha (born 1869 and died 1900 in childbirth) and a son by the name of Peter.

My grandfather Cornelius (Kornelius) John Düek (born 1861 and died 1921) and Margaretha Düek (née Klassen) were married in 1890. Their children were Peter†, John, Maria, and Margaretha†. After the death of my grandmother in 1900, Cornelius John Düek was remarried in 1901 to Susanna Thiessen (born 1875 died 1911). Their children were Henry, Cornelius†, Anna, Cornelius†, and Jacob†.

The Düeks, like the Warkentins, were Dutch Mennonites. In 1905, Kornelius, Susanna and their children were part of the second wave of Dutch Mennonite emigrants. Both families, the Düeks, and the Warkentins thirty years earlier—indeed several entire Mennonite colonies—departed Russia for Canada and the United States because of the Russian government at that time. The Russian Social Democratic Party—later to become the Soviet Communist Party—took over the Russian government in 1796, shortly after the death of Catharine the Great, Empress of Russia. Empress Catherine had given special considerations to the Mennonite colonists by way of incentives to re-settle in South Russia from Poland. These incentives included freedoms of language, education, religion, and exemption from military service. Mennonites were, and still are, for the main part, pacifists. But under the Russian Social Democratic Party, these colonists were scrutinized as interlopers and unwelcome guests, so the special concessions were withdrawn. By 1905, the unrest in the Russian Mennonite colonies increased.

The more rational element of the Russian government, realizing that they would be losing a further 40,000 of their more industrious farmers and tradespeople tried to present a reasonable alternative to the colonies in order to keep them; however the hostile elements of the government prevailed, requiring the colony residents to use the Russian language for all commerce and education activities as well as charging them a heavy monetary tax for their immunity from military service.

And so the second wave of emigrants was now mobilized to depart. My mother's family—Kornelius, her father, Susanna (her stepmother), Henry (her stepbrother), Anna (her stepsister), and John (her brother)—had for several weeks been bidding *Aufscheet* [a Mennonite-Dutch term for final farewells; *it is unlikely we will meet again*] and it was a time of sadness and tears.

Most of the departing families had sold their properties, furniture, and livestock, but it took two months of waiting for their passports to arrive. The current emigrants assembled in Odessa and travelled by train to Hamburg, Germany. A passenger ship was waiting in Hamburg to take them to Southampton, England, and then across the Atlantic Ocean to Montréal. Maria was in the fourth level of schooling. Schools, in general, had their studies and courses in the German language since it was the most developed language used in Northern and Eastern Europe.

Although she was not very old, Maria had made enduring friendships with many of the neighbourhood children. Several Russian men and women employees had housing provided for them and their families on the property owners' land. These workers also had children, so Maria had friends among them as well; in fact, she learned enough of the Russian language through her association with her friends to be able to converse with them. The thought of having to leave her friends troubled her very much. In later years, when she spoke of her childhood to her own children, Maria would recall her Russian girlfriends by name, Olga, Alisa, Vera and Catharine, as well as the Mennonite girls, Anna, Helena, and Christina. She described their appearances and then wept at the thought of never seeing them again. Those departing for the west were leaving friends and family they had known their whole lives and had to come to terms with the fact that, in all likelihood, they would never see them again here on Earth. The people who were leaving had little or no idea where they were going; a lot of trust was placed in their leaders, who had travelled to Canada and the USA prior to deciding to emigrate. What they had found on their investigative trip was that both the Canadian and USA governments welcomed them, assuring the

Mennonite visitors as much land as was needed and that they would provide all the freedoms that had been withdrawn by the Russian government. Those who were staying prayed for the departing, and the departing prayed for those they would be leaving behind. When they met on the streets, they would hesitate for a few moments to comfort each other with biblical confidence that they could put their trust not just in God, who had guarded them, but also in their predecessors who had fled from their beloved Netherlands, and who would now guide them, as was their way. This trust required periodic affirmation, for not long after the Mennonites arrived at their new homes, they received word that the radical faction of the Russian Social Democratic Party had plundered the Mennonite homes and farms, and many of the remaining people had been put to death. This tragedy befell Maria's grandparents and other relatives as well as many of her friends.

TWO

Start of a Long Journey

The train left Odessa, where the emigrants had gathered to embark for the journey to the German port of Hamburg. There were very few dry eyes as the people who were left behind pondered the future of these passengers—while the departing emigrants thought about the possible fate facing their lifetime friends who opted to remain in South Russia.

The train ride was long and tedious. The passenger cars were not built for comfort although they had benches to sleep on and friends with whom to share their sorrows and hopes. Mothers had packed lunches to last them until they embarked their ship. It was early September, and the countryside was alive with farmers bringing in the harvest. These scenes, although picturesque and lively, brought tears to their eyes especially to the adult passengers.

During the trip, several obstacles appeared in the paths of the travellers; for example, upon arriving at Hamburg, the passengers were quarantined for thirty days. In the meantime Anna, who was a month old, developed a fever. The passenger line's doctor, who was on staff in Hamburg, provided medication for her, and although it alleviated the fever, she was still very weak. The time spent in quarantine gave her time to get much of her strength back. While in quarantine, no one was allowed to leave the compound. The travellers' food supplies were exhausted, but the medical mission in the compound provided them with rations that were available. By the time they boarded the ship, the people were glad to be on their way once more. The ship's doctor and his staff examined each of the passengers for signs of illness that might hinder their journey.

The passenger ship sailed for Southampton, England, the following morning. Many emigrants from Britain, who also were waiting for passage to Canada, had assembled in Southampton. Once they set sail for England, Anna became very ill once again. The ship's doctor decided that she and her family would be required to remain in England for Anna's sake because his medical crew would need all their resources for the remaining passengers, in case of an emergency.

The Düek family disembarked in Southampton, and in doing so they missed their trip to Montréal. The Southampton port volunteer staff found accommodation for the family in a nearby home. They stayed there for three weeks, through the kindness of an English family that offered them accommodation for as long as was needed to build up Anna's strength. They had their meals with their hosts, and when it was time to leave and board the next ship to Canada, Kornelius tried to pay for their keep, but the hosts would not accept payment. The Mennonite family was so impressed with British hospitality that Kornelius wondered if they should remain in England rather than go on. The differences in languages might have presented a problem, but the kindness of the British family and the humility of their guests overcame whatever differences were present. Kornelius decided, then and there, to have his family learn the English language as one of their priorities.

THREE

Immigrant Travels

It was early November 1905 when the Düeks boarded the next ship bound for Montréal. It took many days crossing the Atlantic Ocean; they were days of excitement not only for the children but for the adults as well. Some of the crew members gave English language instructions to any who were interested. Then there were information sessions about Canadian geography and the cultural everyday life of the country's residents. Passengers had discussion periods, among themselves, with opportunities to relate what their backgrounds had been prior to emigrating from Southern Russia and what their aspirations and concerns were in establishing their homes in Canada. Kornelius described his occupation in Russia as having been the owner and operator of a flour mill—since Canada, at least what he had learned about the country, had an agriculture base, he felt certain that his skilled experience should be much in demand.

The passenger record listed several tailors, coopers, weavers, carpenters, farm-equipment makers, blacksmiths, mechanics, and of course farmers. The women who did not have children to care for also had experience and training that would help them in the new country. Among the ladies were nurses, two doctors, several office clerks, three general store owner/operators, midwives, and seam-stresses. The thought went through Kornelius' mind that, if these passengers could remain together after disembarking in Montréal, they in themselves might be able to establish a thriving, self-suffi-cient community. It showed that Kornelius was open to a variety of opportunities; farming might not have a very high priority in his mind.

An interesting detail: on the ship's passenger list, males over age fourteen were classed as *labourers* regardless what their skills might have, been ladies of that age group were *spinsters*, unless they were married, in which case they were categorized as *wife*; boys and girls under fourteen were categorized as *child*, while children under two years were listed as *infant*.

Two people, an elderly man and a young child, died on the journey and were buried at sea. Maria remembered the burial services, and in future years she would hear adults talking about the "first casualties" among the immigrants on their way to the New Country.

The passengers voiced many concerns among themselves includ-ing: the ability to learn English; the Indians, about whom they had heard troubling stories; and their ability to properly educate their children—Maria was in her fourth year of schooling. The sheer size of Canada made the prospect of what lay before them daunting. Would they be able to deal with strange customs changes? Would previous immigrants assist them in coping with so many adjustments?

They comforted each other that, so far in their history, their fore-fathers and foremothers had placed their trust in God's guidance, benevolence, and care; this was especially true during the Protestant Reformation period, when the established Roman church hierarchy, forced them to flee their beloved Netherlands for Eastern Europe to practice their new-found faith, and to protect their families from harm. God would now once more provide protection and leadership, seeing them through this critical period; even so, they had periods of doubts. The families met every day for a time of prayer.

The Atlantic Ocean was so vast, so much larger than the lakes with which they had become familiar in Russia, and it seemed at times as though the voyage would never end. Then one day the ship's captain suggested that the passengers look to the west—there was land, barely visible through the mist, but they were nearing land, which brought joy mixed with sadness for the passengers; joy to near their journey's end—sadness because they were so far from their homeland, relatives and friends. As the ship steamed up the St. Lawrence River, the passengers crowded on deck for glimpses of this new country about which they had heard and read; Canada, their new home. Maria was especially excited at the prospect of seeing Canadian Indians, buffalo, modern cities, and the place which would be their home. She had picked up a few English words along the way. Some of them sounded very much like words in their Mennonite Dutch dialect. Even at her young age, she noticed that several words sounded the same in both languages, for example: ship/shepp; wool/w(v)oll; man/maun; pill/pell; farmer/foarma; ball/baul. Maria had been a good student in school; she looked forward to the new challenges that awaited her.

The ship's passengers crowded on deck to get good views of Canada. Many were excited as they spotted villages and towns along the riverbank. Although it was winter, a number of farms came into view, with farmers bringing hay in their barns for winter storage. The children scanned the river banks for Indians, but they could not

J. Edwin Warkentin

distinguish between the original people and immigrants. A few of the more curious children were disappointed at not seeing buffaloes.

FOUR

Arrival in Canada

The ship docked in Montréal in December 5, 1905. The Canadian Customs Department provided Kornelius and his family with an overnight stay in a nearby hotel. It was so good to be on dry land again although there was snow on the ground. They were given dinner that evening and breakfast the following day in the hotel dining room. These would be their first meals on Canadian soil, and although the food was not to what they were accustomed, Kornelius gathered his family together and gave thanks to God for his providence.

The following day, Kornelius and his family had an appointment with Canada Customs, a meeting that would change their lives for decades to come. The customs agent who met with them had been an immigrant himself, from England, so he had compassion for these new arrivals. He had an interpreter who spoke and understood the Low-German language with which Kornelius, although it was not the Mennonite vernacular, could make his way throughout the interview.

"What had you been doing in Russia?" asked the agent.

"I owned and operated a flour mill," he said.

"Do you know anything about farming?"

"I know very little about grain farming," said Kornelius, "and less about domestic animal management."

The agent suggested that, since he had handled grain in making flour, perhaps he might make a try of farming as so many immigrants from Europe had already done. The discussion turned to housing where Kornelius and his family lived. They lived near the flour mill in a two-storey town house, but were ready to attempt whatever the Canadian agent had in mind.

The customs agent went to consult with his manager-agent and explained what this Mennonite family were accustomed to and where they might be best suited. He also discussed what the father should be doing to support his family while at the same time be a productive immigrant. When the agent returned, he gave his opinion, which was that, since Kornelius had dealt with grain, he would likely become a good farmer in Western Canada.

The thought of farming did not appeal to Kornelius at first, so he asked if he might consult with his family. That was permitted, so the parents and their four children went into an adjacent room to discuss with each other about the prospects of farming. The older children, of course, thought it was a great idea, visualizing having their own animals and perhaps even a dog, while their parents spent more time assessing their capability of success having admitted to each other the difficulties that might be ahead. In the end they prayed about their decision to become farmers.

When they gave the customs agent their decision to agree with whatever the Canadian authorities had in mind, he was greatly relieved. The next matter was: where in Canada? The government of Canada was very interested in populating the Prairie Provinces, so with that in mind, land was laid out in 320 acres (130ha) parcels and each eligible settler was allotted one such plot. There were stipulations to which the settler would adhere, such as a certain percentage of the land had to be cleared within five years, the land could not be sold before eight years of occupancy, and a small percentage of finances from marketable produce would be returned to the government each year for eight years. The Canadian government would provide the novice farmer, at his choosing, with a team of animals to do the difficult clearing of land and general farm chores. The farmer would also be given a plough and other farm equipment, a wagon, three cattle, a horse and buggy—horse-drawn vehicle. The government would also provide a house and barn, and a monetary grant of $50 a month for a year.

To be granted so much support almost overwhelmed Kornelius and his wife Susanna. They had not anticipated the generosity of this new country.

FIVE

By Train to a New Home

It came time to inform the family where it would be located. They were to be transported, by train, to the province of Saskatchewan; the exact location was Rush Lake, where a house had been built by a previous owner whose family had returned to England. Rush Lake was a frontier village in south-western Saskatchewan. The trip took four days because the train made stops along the way to let other immigrant families leave. Several were met by relatives who had made the trip a number of years earlier. They included a family of friends of Kornelius and Susanna, from the same part of Russia, who got off the train in Winnipeg, Manitoba, to settle near Winkler, about 85 miles south of Winnipeg.

When Kornelius and his family arrived in Herbert, Saskatchewan, early one morning, they were met by the local government agent who arranged transport for them to their farm in Rush Lake. The transport was a horse and wagon equipped with seats and blankets for the family members and space enough to store their belongings. The trip from Herbert to Rush Lake took two hours.

Rush Lake village consisted of five houses, a small general store, a grain elevator and a train station. The farm was a mile from the village. Their new home, they were told, was on the shores of the lake—more like a swamp. They could not see the water or ice for the rushes [a marsh grass] which grew as far as the eye could see. It is not known what the family had expected for a house, but what they saw was a four-room cottage with smoke coming out of the chimney. Their nearest neighbours, upon hearing that a new family was taking over the property, had cleaned up the house—and even painted two rooms—which previous owners abandoned when the head of that family died. The neighbours supplied the incoming family with sheets, blankets, dishes, pots and pans. They also brought fresh baking to welcome their new neighbours.

The isolated appearance of their new residence came as a shock to Kornelius and Susanna. In fact, it was a moment of, "what have we gotten ourselves into?" The older two children, in the meantime, ran around the house exploring the various rooms, claiming some of them for themselves. Their parents tried their best to communicate with their neighbours, and the neighbours in turn did their best to understand these travellers from a far-away land by trying to comfort and assure them. Maria, although still young, wondered silently, if this move had been a big mistake. There would be many days when that question would come up for both parents. As so frequently happens, the anxieties diminished, but the wisdom—or lack of wisdom—to bring his family into this isolated location troubled Kornelius for months to come.

Much had to be done around the property before winter really set in. The water well for their house and cattle use needed to be cleaned up and sheltered from winter storms. The stable had to be cleaned and made ready for winter. Firewood needed to be cut and stacked in a sheltered place. More furniture would be needed, and

J. Edwin Warkentin

most important of all, the older children must be enrolled in the school. These tasks and many other daily chores occupied Kornelius' time, so the other worries were temporarily put aside, and would be looked after as time passed by.

Susanna, although she did not regret the move to Rush Lake, was still lonely for her parents and friends back in Russia. She was kept busy with her children, but she did miss the conveniences she had six months previously. Once the groceries had been procured, she baked bread, prepared vegetables for meals, cleaned the house, laundered the clothes, patched clothes, and made sure that the children were well cared for. She even made children's clothes using the portable manually operated sewing machine she had brought with her from Russia.

When the district government agent figured that this family had had time to settle down in their new home, he came to see how Kornelius and Susanna were managing, suggesting that Kornelius and he go to the auction in Swift Current to get some animals, a sleigh, animal feed, and some winter clothes for Susanna and the children.

Although neither of the two could speak each other's language, the government agent had considerable experience and patience working with people who had recently arrived. Kornelius was anxious to learn the English language and also to learn from others how things were done in Canada. The government agent was pleased to see how this family had adjusted in such a short time. Before he left, he suggested that his wife and Susanna should go to town and become familiar with the stores. Susanna was pleased with the idea, and she soon made a list of items for the house and for needed winter clothes. She was also excited with the possibility of meeting another woman. Maria enquired of the agent, as best as she could, if he had children. The agent said he had two daughters and two sons about the same age as Maria and her brothers. When the agent left, the family gathered around the kitchen table for prayer—for answered prayer; to help them handle all the daily adjustments, despite their moments of misgivings. Their daily chores kept them busy, taking their minds off potential difficulties, rewarding them with the visible progress being made in their house and farmyard.

SIX

Life on the Farm

Maria and her brother John had been enrolled in the local one-room country school. Some of the school subjects, such as arithmetic and reading, were taught by merging several classes. Most of the families whose children attended school came from different parts of Europe and Great Britain. The teacher took an interest in this immigrant family to the extent that she would visit them on Saturdays with pictures and a mail order catalogue, teaching them English, using pictures and English descriptions.

Several weeks after his last visit, the government immigration agent came by and offered to take Kornelius with him to the Swift Current cattle auction, which had been advertised for that week. Susanna gave her husband a shopping list for necessary items including groceries, hoping he might have time to purchase the necessities. With the prospect of buying two cows and perhaps a horse, the agent had arrived with a sleigh pulled by two horses. The sleigh had a large grain box which could accommodate two cows. If a horse was also purchased it would be tied to the back of the sleigh for the trip home. The idea was for the agent and Kornelius to stay overnight in Swift Current, sleeping in the hayloft attached to the auction sheds, and leave the day after the auction sale for home. The agent had brought blankets with him—through past experience he had become aware of the lack of accommodation in the town and how to deal with it.

The cattle auction went well for Kornelius. He purchased two cows, one that was still being milked and the other one was due to calf within three months. He also bought a young horse which would be used for light work and transportation. He was well pleased with his accomplishment. While the agent went to the local government office to discuss any events or instructions pertaining to his profession, Kornelius shopped at one of the two general stores in town. By the time he finished he had a large box of groceries to carry to the auction office for safekeeping until next day. He then attended to his purchases of that day by ensuring that his livestock had enough water and feed for the night.

The sleep in the hay was something new to Kornelius, but he didn't object since the government agent and several other men from out of town thought nothing of the practice. In fact he found it comfortable enough, and he was thankful for the blankets which the agent had brought with him.

In the morning, all the men got up before dawn, gave their animals enough food to tide them over until they reached home, then they went to a local coffee shop for breakfast. It was just as dawn was breaking that the agent and Kornelius got under way. Their trip home took several hours. Kornelius would check up on the condition of his animals every mile, and would walk for about three miles beside the horse which was tied on the back of the sleigh. Kornelius was elated with the treasures he was bringing home. He was certain that Susanna and the children would welcome the new members of their family. The children had wanted a dog, but that would have to wait until spring.

Even though Maria was eight years old, she was put back into grade one because of her lack of the English language. Her schooling in Russia was similar to the Canadian grading system; the main difference was that her lessons had all been in the German language because many of the textbooks were written in that language. The language spoken at home was Plautdietsch, a Dutch dialect, her schooling language had been in German, her Christian faith language had been mainly Dutch, her conversation with neighbouring children had been in Russian, and now she was learning English, since that was the language both of Canada and the school which she attended. Maria had to put in extra time in school to keep up with the work, which she enjoyed. Since her fellow students spoke only English, she caught on very quickly.

In the spring of 1906, Maria and John helped Susanna plant their garden. The previous owners of their place had cleared a piece of land for a garden, so all Susanna had to do was clean it up and plant seeds; they had some experience in this regard before arriving in Canada. Maria was also busy trying to categorize the various flowers and prairie plants that were abundant at that time of year. She was also very interested in the gophers and small burrowing owls. She caught a small gopher one day, but when it bit her finger, she decided to leave them alone.

Kornelius, who was now forty-six years of age, decided it was time to clear some land and plant a crop of grain. During the winter months, he had read up, with the assistance of the government agent, on how to go about farming in what was, at that time, prairie sod. He was advised to get a two-animal team for cultivating the land.

He knew that oxen were strong, so he bought one—the only one available in the market. To make a team he bought a large, strong horse. Ploughing the sod was slow and tedious. The team he had was mismatched. At first, as he started turning over the turf, the horse and ox seemed to tolerate each other, but as summer wore on, he learned that the two animals were at variance with each other. Maria remembered the many times when her father would relate his experiences trying to get more land ploughed. When the days were hot, the flies came out in swarms, and the ox had a mind of its own. The farm bordered Rush Lake, which was not much more than marsh land, and when the ox decided to slope off into the slough there was little the farmer or the workhorse could do about it; the team, plough and farmer would be dragged along. Needless to say, the farmer was very disconcerted over these events; however, he put up with this way of farming for the first year, after which he sold the ox and bought a second work horse. Kornelius had done fairly well in changing hard prairie sod into arable soil for crop production. The government agent was very pleased and commended Kornelius for his assiduous attitude toward farming. After consulting with the federal agency in Ottawa concerning Kornelius' achievements, the agent was given the authority to forgive Kornelius of the hold the government of Canada might have had on the farm; in other words Kornelius and Susanna were given full title to the land and buildings.

This joy was soon overshadowed in 1911. Susanna suffered during a difficult pregnancy. She became violently ill, resulting in her death in her—thirty-sixth year—and the death of her infant. Kornelius was devastated, and much of his time was taken in persecuting himself for not looking after Susanna carefully enough through the ten years they had been married. There appeared to be a deep-seated

J. Edwin Warkentin

malady in those years that so many infants and or their mothers died during parturition.

SEVEN

Maria and Jacob

Maria was now fourteen. She was expected to quit school and manage the household tasks including making meals, doing the laundry, helping Anna—who was six—and her brothers get ready for school with clean clothes and a lunch. In later years, when she spoke of those days, she never complained but considered it her duty to help her father and his children. She mentioned several times how she had to run the two miles to their nearest neighbours for information when making meals and baking bread.

The year after Susanna died, Kornelius decided to take his family and move to Manitoba, where they had other relatives. In 1912 the family moved to Winkler, Manitoba, where Kornelius bought a small farm on the outskirts of town. Maria and John attended a youth association sponsored by a local Mennonite organization in Winkler. It was there that she met Jacob B. Warkentin from Haskett. After several meetings the two fell in love and were married in June 1918 at Jacob's parents' farm. The J.B. Warkentins had seven children, of which I was the fourth.

Jacob (Jack) was born in 1918. He would go on to serve in the Royal Canadian Air Force during World War Two. After the war, he joined the federal government civil service, and as their representative, he was sent to various countries in the world, assisting the local governments in establishing efficient management working systems. He married Eunice Bower from Ottawa, Ontario.

J.B and Maria's second son, John, was born in 1919 but died in 1921.

Cornelius Henry (Conn), their third, was born in 1921. He too would go on to serve in the RCAF during World War Two as an aircraft systems engineer. After the war he attended the University of Toronto, coming out as a civil engineer working in Canada and the United States. Conn married Gertrude Cook from Newfoundland.

1921 also saw the death of Kornelius; he was chasing some of his cattle through deep grass on the farm outside of Winkler when he tripped and burst some of his internal organs. While he was still conscious, he asked Maria to look after Henry and Anna, and she agreed. Kornelius was sixty-one at the time of his death. Henry and Anna came to live with Maria and J.B. until they were capable to fend for themselves.

Peter was born in 1925. He too would serve in the RCAF both during World War Two and in peacetime as an engineering officer with the rank of Captain. Peter married Evelyn Staten in 1945; she died in 2006. He would go on to marry Lillian Cornelius in 2007.

Doris born in 1926 and would became a medical records stenographer for the Vancouver General Hospital. Doris would marry Benny Reed, who died in 1987.

Reginald was born in 1932 and would spend his adult years in the Royal Canadian Signals Corps, serving in Germany, during the Middle East conflicts, and other military bases in North America. Reg would rise to the rank of Major. He would marry Gail Robins;

she died in 1993. He would then marry Hilde Tewes of Barrie, Ontario, in 1996. Reginald died in October 2012.

Over the years, mother and father moved several times until they found a farm which suited their expectations—it was located just on the outskirts of Morden, Manitoba. Although the soil was very good, it was full of rocks as was evidenced by the rows of stones which father had placed along the fences. I was three years old when we moved to that farm, and we lived there until I was nine, so I got to know and remember the farmyard layout, especially the house, which had two stairways to the upstairs bedrooms.

The town butchers from Morden had an abattoir near our barn; attached to it was a corral where the cattle, sheep and pigs were held, waiting their turn to be killed. I recall the terrible screams as they were led onto the killing floor. To see what was going on I would sit on the top rail of the corral, but I did not understand the process; whatever it was, it was a terrible experience for a youngster.

Our land also bordered a cemetery. Some days I would hang around the fence separating our farm from the burial grounds and wonder why so many people were weeping. One day, after the people had left the cemetery, I climbed through the fence and saw a nice bouquet of flowers on the ground. Thinking that someone had just thrown them on the ground, I took them to mother. She had me take them back, straight away.

J. Edwin Warkentin

EIGHT

Early Education

In September of 1930, at seven years of age, I started school at the Morden Maple Leaf Elementary. I was unable to start school at six because of a physical weakness brought on by rheumatic fever at an earlier age, which resulted in me having to learn to walk once again. I had so looked forward to attending school. My Aunt Anna Mary made a school bag—today it would be a backpack—for my precious school items; father bought a pencil box with three new pencils and a work book. I was so pleased that I might be able to read and write in a few days. That dream soon vanished because what I had not been prepared for was that the school was conducted in English; our language at home was a Dutch dialect.

To be in grade one was a thrill beyond measure. However, an incident that came before the end of September caused me a lot of concern. The teacher, Miss Powell, had sketched a grid on the black-board with the pupils' names in alphabetical order down one side and many vacant squares opposite each name. The vacant squares would receive coloured chalk stars every time the student achieved a skill. At some point, unbeknownst to me, someone had placed an unearned star opposite my name. After recess the teacher called me

27

up to her desk and asked why I had done that. Of course, I had *not* done that, but my English was too limited for me to explain my innocence. She did not believe me, so she took the strap out of her desk drawer and walloped me stinging blows on both hands, right in front of the class—perhaps as an object lesson for the other students, but also to give vent to her impatience. When I went home that day and tried to explain what had happened, father assumed I had done something wrong, so he beat me up too. In later years that might have turned me off education, but in grade one, I knew that nothing was going to deter me from learning to read and write. That incident also marked the start of a stammer which persisted until I was forty-four years old, standing before my own class of 250 students, teaching electrical engineering subjects at the British Columbia Institute of Technology; at that time the stammer just vanished, perhaps because of my fright of the moment or more likely because I had asked God to please help me. The dean and chief instructor who interviewed me for the teaching position noted my speech hesitation while groping for words that did not require a stammer. The dean told me not to worry about it, in fact, he said I should take advantage of it—how, I did not know.

In 1933 our utopian lifestyle came to an abrupt stop; the great depression arrived with a vengeance. Father had a bank mortgage on our farm. Although the farm was sufficient to feed our family, it did not bring in enough money to make mortgage payments. The result was that the sheriff would appear monthly to take away a horse, a couple of cows or some farm implements. In order to keep things together as much as possible, father took to cutting trees in some of our wooded areas—these were mainly oak and ash—which he sold in town for firewood. One of the problems of that venture was

J. Edwin Warkentin

that the customers did not have any more finances than we did. In 1934 we lost the farm altogether, so a crucial move had to be made. Grandfather Warkentin came up with a plan for our family to move to an abandoned farm near Gladstone, Manitoba, a distance of about 75 miles. In some of my youthful acrimonious reminiscences, I have believed it was a move to get us far enough away so that father, mother and we six children would be out of sight and out of mind. This was possibly the most depressing and mind-searing time in the lives of our family—it certainly was for me. Jack went to stay with our grandparents for the first winter so that he could finish his grade ten education, while the rest of us started to reconstruct our lives on a ramshackle farm at Golden Stream.

Our one-room school which the four of us attended—Reg was only two at the time—was a mile and a half from our farm. We walked every school day come hail or high snowdrifts. We moved there in October 1934, when I was in grade four. For grades four, five and six I was the lone student in those grades. The teacher taught grades one to eight, but then she also had to assist the eight high school students who sat at the back of the room, taking their courses by correspondence. I often wondered how she coped with so many grades to attend to every day. I have also wondered how the senior students could complete their chemistry and physics studies without any associated lab experiment equipment. The school did not have a library, in fact there were no books except for a partial set of 1911 Books of Knowledge stacked up on the floor Some of the older boys would come to school directly from cleaning their barns. The teacher would say, "I smell animals," which meant that students were to go out and clean their boots.

Frequently our family was so poor that we often took lard and onion sandwiches to school for lunch. Thankfully, the bread was wholesome, and we had lots of milk. I do not remember any of us being sick, except in the summer of 1935, when I had a reoccurrence of rheumatic fever; it was a good thing that the health problem happened during the summer holidays, for I did not miss any school time. In the winter, many students brought potatoes and baked them on the central heater.

My older brothers were assigned many of the farm duties. We had only three horses remaining so they had to do the heavy lifting. Our family transport was a wagon made on the chassis and wheels off a discarded car. Speaking of cars, father had brought his 1928 Ford Model "T" touring car with us which he stored it in a shed for two years. I saw him on several occasions go into the shed and tinker with anything which would ensure its good running order when the time would come to move away. I asked him in later years if that had been his intention; he replied in the affirmative.

Our farm was six miles from the town of Gladstone. Most of our groceries were paid for by bartering fresh butter and eggs at the local grocery store for sugar, flour, salt, oatmeal and soap. Father tried to make cooked ground-up wheat for an alternative cereal, but it took a lot of chewing and needed another ingredient to make it edible, so we made do with oatmeal. Each week one of us would appointed to the role of butter churner; mother would fill the little butter press with butter, wrap each pound in butter paper and then put the packages in a cool place until our next trip into town. At home coffee was replaced by *prips,* roasted, ground rye grain from our granary. No doubt this was a healthy drink, but it had very little taste. Mother was given discarded overalls from some of the neighbours. She would unstitch and wash the pieces then make clothes for us on her old treadle sewing machine, which she had received in 1918 as a wedding gift. She made our underwear from flour sacks. She must have dreamed up the style because they did not resemble clothes of any sort you might see in clothing stores; but they covered the essentials. In winter we were given new fleece lined underwear from Eaton's catalogue, with the indispensable trap door at the back. In summer we went in bare feet most of the time, but in winter we wore several layers of socks in moccasins. During snow blizzards in the winter, father would take us to school and back with horses and sleigh.

We had a big garden that kept us in enough vegetables until the following summer. Mother would preserve beans, peas, corn and pickles. She also made a kind of marmalade from citron melons and rhubarb. When I think back, our meals must have been the healthy type; we seldom saw candies and never fast foods.

My brother Peter and I herded the cattle in the summer so they would not stray. Fences that had once been there were there no more. Our farm must have been on an earlier aboriginal settlement because we found many arrowheads and other items made from stone. During our first summer on that location, we hunted gophers for the bounty of one cent for each tail. We had enough action to buy each of us a pair of running shoes. Those shoes protected our bare feet from thistles, stubble and odds and ends in a farm yard.

During our stay at Golden Stream, one of the grain companies built an elevator right by the railway tracks. Father was hired to help see the project through. The work took all summer. The income did see us through another fall and winter.

There came day in early October 1936, father announced that, the following week, we would be moving to Portage la Prairie. I do not know how he did it, but he had found a house for rent for ten dollars a month, a house that had been taken over by the city because the previous owner could not pay his property taxes. The possibility of moving into a town conjured up possible happenings about which one could only dream. My older brothers were assigned to load the hay wagon with our meagre belongings, put the chickens in coops on top, tie a cow to the back of the wagon, and then drive this Gypsy-like procession to Portage la Prairie. Father had sold all the cattle but one.

The morning we left for Portage la Prairie. Father drove the Model T out of the shed; on a piece of cardboard, he printed—IN TRANSIT—and fastened it to the front grill in place of a license plate. Then he and mother and the four of us children piled in, and we were off. The distance from what was then Golden Stream—that place like others no longer exist—to Portage la Prairie was about thirty miles or just under sixty kilometres.

Life in a town was very different from slaving away on a farm, which had gone to seed by the previous owner, because of the drought, grasshoppers, gophers and dust storms. We had lost most of our farming machinery during the debacle of our previous farm. Now we had sidewalks, street lights and stores nearby. Father found a job at the local mental hospital farm. His responsibility was to supervise the farm work. Because some of the patients were required to do help with the farm work, tractors or other motorized equipment were not allowed. Father had a lot of experience with horses, which worked in his favour. One of his responsibilities in the spring and summer was to harness four horses and make them ready to work in the fields. Jim, one of the residents at the farm, was to help with the horses. By the time father had harnessed the third horse Jim had taken the harness off the first horse and hung it up. This type of problem happened frequently; in fact, father thought this was the most difficult part of his workday.

When World War Two broke out, father was hired as a stationary engineer at the RCAF station near MacDonald airport. He rode his bicycle there and back every working day, even though the fifteen miles was a gravel highway.

My first day at Portage la Prairie Central School was an eye-opener, for Portage la Prairie was the third largest city in Manitoba at the time, with a population approaching 12,000 (if you included dogs). I, as a forlorn looking child with a stutter, went to the principals' office, and after she had read my report card from Golden Stream School, she took me to the grade six classroom. The scene that met me came as a shock—an entire room full of grade six students. I was then introduced to Miss Hall and the thirty-six students as "the farm boy who now wished to live in a city." The transition from a one-room school to a one-room grade-six classroom was, at first, difficult for me to take in; the immediate setting jangled my nervous system, causing my stammer to get worse. I had long ago, in fact by the end of grade one, overcome the English barrier in my daily living to the point I had learned to think in English although, when speaking, my mind was busy searching for synonyms that did not necessitate a stutter. Now the time had come for me to merge with the grade six class and catch up to what I had missed in the past six years.

Marjorie Hall was everything that a teacher should be. She did not single me out as a new arrival but rather included me in whatever activities were presented. I loved her from the start, not only because of her kind spirit, although that surpassed all others, but that she introduced me, with the rest of the class, of course, to the school library and then to the city library. I had thought there might be such organizations, but seeing them almost overwhelmed me; so many books. The first book I read was *Call of the Wild* by Jack London; my second book was *Robinson Crusoe* by Daniel Defoe. In later years I once again read *Robinson Crusoe* which brought back happy memories.

Then too Miss Hall introduced the class to classical and contemporary music, using a gramophone. Of course, listening to the music instilled in me a lasting appreciation for music although I never became proficient at playing an instrument. During the art classes, she would give each student an art card copy of the picture painting we would study that day along with a biography of the artist. These classroom events have stayed with me all my life, and I have been grateful for having Miss Hall as a teacher.

Those were times when I started daydreaming, a habit which has not entirely left me to this day. Another personal incident that endeared Miss Hall to me occurred just before Christmas, when teachers would take their class to the local theatre to see a movie of interest to children. At noon, when I went home for lunch, I told my parents that the afternoon school schedule would include a movie at the theatre. For one reason or another they would not allow me to go to the picture show, but I would have to go and tell the teacher my parents would not permit me to go. It was a trying experience for me, but I did it and instead of questioning me for the reason— even now I would be hard-pressed to give one—she gave me a dime and sent me home. That was the first money I had for my very own; I bought an embroidered handkerchief for mother for Christmas.

About fifty years later, when my wife and I travelled by car from Vancouver to Winnipeg and then Toronto on holiday, we passed through Portage la Prairie. I just had to find out if Miss Hall was still in town. The city clerk showed me the voters list for the previous year, and there she was, living in a seniors' residence. I went to see her and introduced myself, but she said she knew who I was as soon as she saw me. We hugged each other and shed many tears, at least I did, thanking her for kindnesses and introductions to what the whole world had to offer to a lonely farm boy in 1936. At one point she remembered that I had a "mischievous disposition." Miss Hall died the following year; she was ninety years old.

I must include an incident which frightened me greatly—as it did most of the boys in grades six and seven. Portage la Prairie had the province's detention centre for wayward boys who had been caught committing crimes. The man who kept them in line had been a regimental sergeant-major (RSM) from the First World War. He was a stern disciplinarian, over six feet tall and very tough in his demeanour. Well, every Wednesday afternoon, grades six and seven boys knew that this soldier would arrive, in full army uniform with medals gleaming and give us military drill with wood rifles and marching in unison. His other job was to receive, from the principal, Miss Moore, a strap and a list of boys who had misbehaved the week before. The soldier would then call them out and viciously strap them on both hands and wrists in front of the rest of us. Of the audience, some would wet their pants while others just stood there in horror, depending on their holding power. Some of the tougher chaps would openly challenge him to break them down. The RSM had other methods of torture for them, such as having the culprit stand for fifteen minutes with his arms outstretched, palms down and the RSM's gold pocket watch placed on one of their hands. When I enlisted in the RCAF during World War Two I suspected everyone with a rank above corporal to be as mean as this individual. It turned out, for the main part, not true.

In September 1938 the new grade eight students went across the street and became high school students at the Portage Collegiate Institute. I was now fifteen and had started to form opinions of my own although I kept them pretty well to myself for the time being. When I returned to PCI many years later for the school's 100th Anniversary, I looked up the students paper of 1938, *The Tattler*, under my name the editor had written: "When Eddie started in grade eight, the teachers looked up books on child psychology." Not a nice thing to say about me.

Several memorable events happened while I was in grades nine and ten. We had teachers with academic specialties who came to our room to teach. One was Miss Stanger, who taught history. She had come, maybe a century earlier, from the Orkney Islands north of Scotland. Miss Stanger resembled Boadicea, Queen of Britain, from images I had seen and read in my history textbook. Warrior Queen Boadicea fought the Roman invaders in the first century AD. She, that is Miss Stanger, was so patriotic that she had the class stand up and sing, *God Save the King* every time she came into our room.

One day, to liven things up a bit, I bumped the backs of the knees of the girl in front of me. Maggie fell down, the *King* stopped in the middle of a bar, and a bellow came from Miss Stanger to **SIT**. I had done this dastardly deed without consideration or the possible consequences. Miss Stanger picked up her pointer (hand–hewn

J. Edwin Warkentin

from a two by four or small tree) from her desk and made a beeline for me waving the weapon as she came. I had seen her beat other mischievous boys, so I knew that my execution was about to take place. Just as she swung the pointer at my shoulder I ducked, she hit my desk which shattered her cudgel into slivers. Had she connected, my right arm could easily have become detached from my shoulder. Instead she, quivering with rage, ordered me to appear in her home room after school for a week and write out five hundred times each day that I would be, from then on, a loyal Canadian. By the end of the week there was no doubt where my loyalties lay. A few years later, when I arrived at home in my air force uniform, I visited the high school, Miss Stanger in particular, to apologize for my youthful misbehaviour. She hugged me in front of her class, which for her was quite a concession, telling students what a loyal Canadian looked like.

Another incident occurred when I was in grade ten. We had to take two languages, Latin and French. The Latin teacher, Miss Webster, informed our class during the first week in September that we were already three weeks behind in Latin from where we should be; the only solution was that we were to remain after classes until we caught up. At first I thought for sure she was kidding, so I did not remain after classes—she was not fooling as I soon found out. She made me leave the room upon her arrival for the rest of the term. The principal, Mr. Garret—also known as "The Beak"—upon seeing me in the cloakroom, asked what I was doing there. After I told him, he just shook his head and left. My colleagues would supply me with the lessons and assignments. I had glued my ear to the hinges side of the door for the term, and either I was very attentive or Miss Webster felt that she had made her point because I passed the Christmas exam, and she let me back into the classroom for the next term. In spite of my mischievous attitude and its consequences, I have always liked Latin.

In my final exams in grade ten, my mark for English Literature was 48 which resulted in me failing the whole year in every subject. So in September 1940, I started grade ten all over again. Of course, I still had all my notes from the previous year, so I was far ahead of most of the new students in the class. In those days we had class "standings." I came in first throughout the year—until May 1941 when I quit school out of boredom.

NINE

Joining the Royal Canadian Air Force

Some students, including me, thrived on Canadian history together with the national anthems which at that time were *The Maple Leaf Forever* and *God Save the King*. Our family, throughout my youth, always lived in predominantly English communities. One of their objectives was, as soon as possible, to integrate with communities that had welcomed them and their parents. It was not surprising then, when World War Two came along, that four of us brothers joined the Royal Canadian Air Force. Reg, who was seven years old when the war broke out, joined one of the army units when he was old enough. He retired with the rank of Major.

After I quit school without finishing grade ten, I worked for a while in a grocery store with Sterling Lyon who worked there after school—he would go on to become premier of Manitoba. Just before I enlisted, I worked for a year at the Air Navigation School, South Airport at Portage la Prairie; that is where I had my first airplane ride.

My schooling did not interest me at that time, so when an RCAF team of recruiters appeared in our town. I was ready to go; go anywhere. In the spring of 1941, with birth certificate in hand, I approached the sergeant's desk expecting a uniform and attendant accoutrements. When the sergeant looked at my birth certificate he said, "Get lost kid (only with more offensive words), come and see us when you're old enough to shave." I was seventeen years old, and the disappointment must have shown because a year later a telegram came to our home asking me to report to the RCAF recruiting office in Winnipeg. The sergeant must have noted my name and address. My parents were a bit reluctant to offer another son for Canada's military service; their two older sons had already enlisted in the Royal Canadian Air Force. The bus ride to Winnipeg on June 22, 1942, was the start of something that would change my life forever.

My previous immature attitude toward education came back to haunt me. Lack of high school graduation prevented me from joining the RCAF as an aircrew member. It was only several years later, after having been in the air force, that flying as a crew member came my way.

One of the first steps toward enlistment was to take off all my clothes and stand naked with about ten other recruits, waiting for a medical officer's thorough but rather invasive inspection. My rheumatic fever had run its course, so now my medical state was A1; however, no uniform— it would be issued later on while finishing our basic military training. Several young fellows including me were given aptitude tests to find out where we would be best suited. My lot fell in with the electronics group—wireless operator ground. A fresh course was to start the following week. In the meantime, all of us who lived out of Metro Winnipeg had to find a place for board and room. My "home" was about fifteen minutes by bicycle to the school to which I was assigned. My bicycle had come with me. While waiting for classes to start, there was much exploring to be done in Winnipeg. This was my first experience of freedom from giving an account of my daily activities; now, freedom—yippee!

Monday came with the first day of courses. Classes were preceded by introductions to the facility, discipline, class hours and last of all the men in white shop coats, the instructors. Up until then, my hobby had been crystal set radios, with headphones, so the possibility of finding out more about electronics intrigued me. As an aside, we had a battery-operated radio in our home; the tubes' filaments which were also the cathodes of the tubes had their own battery which was a lead-acid type, like a car battery, and had to be charged at a shop once its energy ran down. On this one occasion I wanted to listen to a certain program, so I went to the local railway shop where I knew the mechanics had some old dry cell batteries available for the asking. I connected about six in series and connected them to the radio. Although the dry cells did not have much power it was enough to burn out every tube in the radio. It was time for me to learn more about radios and how they worked.

Our class of trainees was divided up into Wireless Electrical Mechanic (WEM) and Wireless Operator Ground (WOG). The latter group was for me because, not only did the topic appeal to me, but the possibility of eventually becoming an aircrew member was a goal to which one could aspire. The instructors were civilian technicians, so the military authority had not as yet set in; that was to come later. The RCAF paymaster appeared once a month with money with which we paid our room and board—with a little left over for the penny-ante gamblers, cigarette smokers, tooth paste, chocolate bars and soft drinks. Some of us had never seen so much money at any one time. The courses comprised mathematics up to trigonometry and introduction to calculus levels, report writing, radio theory, English language and grammar, electronic circuit trouble shooting including lab work on equipment. This program was as different from high school studies as day is to night.

The program's length was five months, after which our class was given train tickets to Montréal—with further transportation, in a large truck, to Lachine, a suburb of Montréal—for basic training. This was my first ride of such length on a train, and my first trip east of Winnipeg. The trip through Northern Ontario was tedious, but the linen tablecloths, the silver dinner service and the meals in the dining car made up for it. Along the way we picked up more armed forces recruits, two of my high school buddies, now navy recruits, were among them.

The introduction to military life was a bit of a jolt, especially for *this* farm boy. We arrived at the Lachine basic training base at 1100 hrs on November 11, 1942.

The schedule was well organized. First of all we were told which barrack building was to be our home for the next month, then we were told to FALL IN out on the road. I wasn't clear on how do you do that; needless to say the orders bellowed at us could have used some clarification but none were forthcoming. Our Flight 33—a term used to identify us—had a date with the medical officer for inoculations, then the barber, then the dentist. Eventually several officers including the medical officer had us corralled in the drill hall for pep talks. I had never been inoculated or vaccinated, so this was a new experience for me; it was not supposed to hurt but my needles must have been dull because they did hurt. The barber gave each one of us the same hairstyle—short all around. The date with the dentist was a very hurtful experience. I had never been to a dentist, so what was about to happen was troubling. The dental assistant examined my teeth and exclaimed, "Dis hairman 'as cavity in 'is toot." The dentist then examined his drills—looking for an especially for a dull one—and the assistant sat on what might have been a bicycle in earlier days and started pedalling so the dentist's drill was now activated. The three of us, dentist, assistant and I had not heard of pain-dulling injections in the gums, so the drilling continued with excruciating agony—for me. Eventually he must have found what he was looking for. The hurt was so bad that the dentist shoved my head between my knees—a feat that was possible in my earlier years—thinking, *this chap was about to pass out.* He immediately broke an ammonia ampoule under my nose, my head snapped back as if on a spring, and my tooth was repaired. The dental personnel were Canadian Army personnel. Needless to say, the care of my teeth took on a high priority after that.

We were taught how to march, how to tell our left foot from the right foot, whom to salute (commissioned officers) and how it was done, whom to not salute (warrant officers and below in rank), how to polish our brass buttons and shoes, how to keep our uniforms (finally we were issued with uniforms!) tidy and pressed, and just general proper deportment. The meals were nourishing, but some of us were not accustomed to having maple syrup poured over everything on the plate at breakfast time. We had a dry canteen and a wet canteen on the site. The wet canteen was for beer drinkers; its atmosphere was foul, so my first and last visits lasted just long enough to get out. The dry canteen sold pop, chocolate bars, socks, toothpaste and other incidentals. We were given a cloth bag which held needles, thread, spare buttons of the metallic and plastic types, depending where they were needed, the bag was called House Wife—not very politically correct by today's standards. Three shirts with six detachable collars were also part of the pack. The underwear issued reminded me of the flour-sack underwear mother used to make. Then there were the fatigue clothes which we put on to do chores, especially pots and pans chores in the kitchen if we were caught doing something not in the King's Regulations (Air) book.

Our pay was $39 dollars a month. We were encouraged to send half of it home so that we might have a bit of capital for adjusting to civilian life if and when the time came. One of the tricks for trapping anyone who did not like doing outside chores was to ask if anyone had a driver's license. There always were those who tried to get out of chores, but these would be assigned to driving wheelbarrows loaded with rubbish.

The medical officers (MOs) had several sessions with his explicit videos showing scenes of venereal diseases and their consequences. The terms used and their injuries were totally foreign to me, but the message took root. Toward the end of our confined to barracks (CB'd) we were allowed out of the camp for the weekend. A friend from a town near to our last farm joined me in "doing the town," as it were. We took the streetcar to downtown Montréal, booking a room in a rather select hotel. For dinner these big time operators went to the hotel's dining room. After dinner we returned to our room finding two *ladies of the night* reclining on our beds. One of them, upon seeing our unease said, "Come 'ere you Hinglish mans and we will show you someting you 'ave navver seed with your heyes."

J. Edwin Warkentin

It did not take these rookies long to remember the films on venereal diseases, and it took little time to arrive at the registration desk to report our guests. The clerk, smirking, told us to take a short walk down the street, and he would take care of the situation. We did that; upon returning to our room the guests were gone.

It was getting near Christmas time. We were now enrolled in Number One Wireless School, located in a former School for the Blind residence in Montréal. The building was spotlessly white-tiled. The air force students were accommodated in rooms of eight people each. With introductory wireless type courses under way, we were told we could go home for the Christmas season, but if anyone returned late, they would be doing pots and pans for some time to come. It was at least two days by train to my home while others living near the West Coast would need even more time. We had ten-day passes and travel vouchers for our journey. My agenda while at home was to show off my uniform for the guys that were still around home, visiting my former teachers, especially Miss Stanger, and skating with some of the young people—for me the young lady was June. We had written letters to each other since I had been away. I was too dense and romantically inexperienced to deal with the possibilities.

The time allotted me had nearly run out, so to avoid the pots and pans detail for coming back late, we said our farewells. I got on the train with mixed feelings, but I was looking to the future with more enthusiasm. The night we left for Montréal a snow storm had blocked the rails through the mountains, so the pots and pans brigade was dutifully employed for several weeks.

The wireless courses we took up were trouble-shooting faulty equipment, Morse code, semaphore signals and the Aldis lamp, used mainly for signalling from ship to ship as long as they were within line of sight. The semaphore was a method of communicating using signalling flags. Perhaps the Morse code was the most difficult to learn; it was like learning a new language but it would be vitally important in my future employment. Of course, being a military unit, there were many parade square activities and long route marches. One might have thought that coming from the prairies we could withstand the Quebec winter climate, but in spite of putting on sweaters, uniforms, scarves, great coat and gloves, and winter caps many of us—including me—nearly shivered to death. The reason was the damp cold penetrated whatever we were wearing. The shivering part probably kept the blood from freezing.

It was at the wireless school that I saw many movies, the first movies for me. The sports section of the school provided us with skis, so we did some cross country skiing during our stay in Montréal. An incident happened when several of us were going to a National Hockey League game at the Forum. The night was bitterly cold when a street car came to where we were waiting for it. The street car stopped, the operator opened the door and quickly closed it. We assumed he had not seen us so I rapped on the door, breaking the glass. A policeman was standing nearby; seeing the problem came over to investigate. The tram operator pointed at me as the culprit. The policeman got his book out to record the happenings when one of our group, an airman second class (AC2) like the rest of us, told the policeman that he was an Air Commodore Second Class and he advised everyone to forget the whole incident. The policeman thought that a good idea, so we proceeded to the game without further incidents—Montrèal defeated Detroit. I met that "Air Commodore 2nd Class" in Edmonton years later when he was a production manager for the CBC sports televising a CFL football game and I was a systems engineer for the Alberta Government Telephones providing the video signal from the football stadium to the microwave system across Canada.

The time came for final tests along with postings. One of the examinations was to test our procedure and wireless understanding under near-active conditions. Several rooms were equipped to simulate radio stations while others made to believe they were aircraft out on patrol. My tests went so well, presumably, that an instructor's position was offered; this did not appeal to me since I wanted to be where aircraft were involved. We were asked where our preference for a posting might be—my choice was for overseas as were several others in our class. The time came when we were told to pack up our kit bags and smile, smile, smile because we were to assemble in Halifax for onward postings by ship.

TEN

Overseas (and Back Again)

Halifax "Y" Depot was the assembly point for all airmen from Canada and from the British Commonwealth of Nations who had trained in Canada and were scheduled to go overseas. While waiting for our call, I went to a local hockey game. Upon returning to "Y" Depot I could hear what sounded like chopping wood by the parade square. When I got closer it was indeed wood being chopped—some of the Australians were cutting down the flagpole with the commanding officer's personal pennant still fluttering; they were using a fire axe from one of the barracks. In the morning, during the assembly of all the troops on the parade square for daily roll call, the CO was in a fit-type rage regarding the defilement of the flagpole with his ensign still attached. After his second query as to the culprits' recognition, the entire Australian company stepped forward. The CO informed them that he would find a ship that day to take them away. He added, "And if I am unable to find a ship I shall buy enough canoes in Halifax and ship you out." Later that day we noticed numerous trucks arriving empty and going full of Aussies.

Our time finally came to embark on to a small merchant vessel, the SS Lady Rodney, at anchor in Bedford Basin near Halifax. A large convoy had been assembled, our ship joined that fleet. We were allocated our sleeping quarters and meals schedules. One of our number, who had been the pianist for a dance band in Port Arthur, Ontario, spotted a piano and pounded out a mean boogie woogie jazz number. The *bos'n* [boatswain: a man who is in charge of the ships discipline, similar to a sergeant-major on a land military base] roared into view, slammed the piano shut, locked it and berated us as immature halfwits who had many lessons to learn.

"If I hear as much as a *fart* from any of you for the rest of this trip, you're for the brig."

Apparently sounds like that mean boogie woogie jazz number could be picked up by German U-boats up to 50 miles away.

Our trip across the Atlantic Ocean passed through the patrol alley of many German U-boat squadrons. We were escorted by a flotilla of corvettes, minesweepers and aircraft which patrolled our passageway to the British Isles. My meals were few and far between because, in January, the North Atlantic was severely turbulent. What we former land lubbers did eat was often unceremoniously passed on to the fish.

Ice formed on cables; normally one inch, they were now four or more inches in diameter. Our voyage was very slow because of the violent weather but also because of the slowness of freighters who were carrying vital supplies to Britain. Eventually we saw land, Ireland, which raised our spirits considerably; only to be shattered the next day when we were informed our ship was to join a convoy going west. Our hopes were raised several days later when we once more sighted land, Newfoundland. A day later we left the convoy and were now on our own until we arrived in St. John's harbour. Troop ships, except for the Queen Mary, were not permitted to travel, large distances by themselves, so they were embedded in convoys. My arrival, although of little consequence to everyone else, would prove to become the most important and happy part of my life.

Our barracks were not completed, so we had to find homes that would accommodate us. My search landed me with a St John's couple at Rawlins Cross, who gave up their living room to me. The house did not have central heat—or any other type of heat—but the landlady gave me a few sticks of kindling and several lumps of coal for the fireplace. All airmen worked shifts so that when my evening shift was over the thought of building a fire to keep warm did not appeal, so it was into bed with lots of covers. In a few months our barrack block was ready for us. We had eaten our meals in the air force mess hall so now the living and eating facilities were close together. This tranquility lasted about six months, until the first detachment of RCAF Women's Division airwomen (WDs) arrived. At that point we had to search for quarters elsewhere again since the airwomen took over the barracks. Two of us were fortunate to find living quarters in a house across the street from the residential part of No. 1 Group Headquarters; the working operations headquarters for No. 1 Group was a mile away. The Air Officer Commanding was Air Vice-Marshal F.V. Heakes; I was to get to know him somewhat better in a few months.

The wireless operating section was next to the operations room. Our communications were point-to-point with London England, Gibraltar, Ottawa, Azores, Halifax, Goose Bay and several outposts around Newfoundland. The primary concern was monitoring the air patrol frequencies. Aircraft patrolling North Atlantic waters were looking for U-boats. Up until the time they sighted a U-boat the air patrol aircraft were ordered to maintain radio silence; they would receive directions from operations through us. Every transmission was crypto-graphed. When a U-boat was sighted, the aircraft would break silence with SM SM SM, their location, and their aircraft identity. Operations would be notified by our shift supervisor and instructions would be passed on to the aircraft crew by radio operators like myself. Numerous times U-boats were sighted, attacked and sunk. We, as radio operators, wore headphones while on duty. The static was often overwhelming, especially if the incoming signal was weak and atmospheric conditions were powerful. My ears took a beating in those days (and nights) which resulted in me now using hearing aids.

Eventually the Fighter Control Operations located at Cape Spear (the easternmost land in North America) was closed down and the operators merged with the operations command centre in St. John's. The airwomen who had worked at Cape Spear were moved to No. 1 Group Headquarters. For several months a certain airwoman worked next to me in the radio room. We came to know each other, what with close work location, dinner dates and long walks. Marjorie Russell, a Fighter Control Operator, from Edmonton and I were engaged in April 1944 to be married in August 1944. Once that was established, we had much to catch up on each other's background, likes and dislikes, having to face both her parents and mine, where the wedding would take place, not to mention details such as where we would live after the war as well as what each of us would do once the war was over. Come to think of it, not all those plans came to completion. At the time we had to live for the moment because, as it turned out, our military superiors had their say before our plans would see completion. To cover up my stammer, I told Marjorie that my nationality was Greek and that I did not speak English very well. Before we were married, I had to confess that I was not Greek at all, and I had done it to cover up my lack of conversation; for several years she referred to me as her Greek!

ELEVEN

Charlottetown

A month after we were engaged, my posting came for No. 2 Air Navigation School, Charlottetown, PEI. The RCAF had decided to use the experience of "ground" radio operators as regular aircrew, in place of Wireless Air Gunners (WAG) who would then be joining operation squadrons for tours over Europe. This was my opportunity to fly as aircrew. We had also to do duty on the ground radio station to become familiar with both sides of the operations. The air force station had been turned over to the Royal Air Force under the British Commonwealth Air Training Plan. The commanding officer was a Royal Air Force (RAF) group captain. Many of the instructors, staff and maintenance service men were RAF. There would come a time when the group captain would, in effect, end my military career, which had possibilities not only at that time but also during post-was service time, to stop any promotions above that of corporal. While stationed in St. John's, I was twice permitted to fly on patrols from Torbay RCAF Unit as an auxiliary radio operator with No. 5 BR squadron flying Canso aircraft.

My problem with the Commanding Officer happened this way: aircrew at that time were flying four days (not continuously) and then were given four days off. For one of those four days off with an additional weekend pass, I was provided with a six day pass. There was quite a bit of planning for our wedding that had not been done. Communication in those days was by letter, which, during wartime, was very slow partially because all mail had to pass the censor. If anything happened while away to prevent me reporting for duty in time, some of my colleagues who were on days off would take my place. It was common knowledge among my contemporaries what my plans were.

My plan was to fly to Moncton from Charlottetown by Maritime Central Airways then to Torbay (St. John's airport) by service aircraft. This all worked well, with only one day of my six was used up with transportation. Marjorie had a list of things to be done. She had written to her aunt in Saint Lambert, Quebec, for cloth with which to make her wedding dress. My letter to her father for his permission to marry his daughter was composed and sent off. He replied by return mail to say he consented but he would expect that his daughter would be given the lifestyle with which she had been raised. Marjorie laughed that one off since her father at times did not even know her name: is it Margaret, Madge, Margery, or even Marjorie ?—when it came to income tax time. Where we would go on our honeymoon and other important matters were on the list. We spent the next day shopping, followed by a dinner in one of the posh restaurants in St. John's. We took great pleasure in designing our future. Both of us were very happy. These activities took up the next day. My preparations were to leave the third day, so the adjutant had provided me with a travelling warrant to go back to Moncton by service aircraft. Then disaster; fog rolled in, which meant there would be no flying; in fact there was no flying by either the North

Atlantic Patrols or by service aircraft to Canada. I faced two dilemmas. The first was not getting back to Canada on time. The second was the possibility of facing the RAF commanding officer, who let it be known he did not like the RCAF, its airmen, or even their aircraft. I asked for permission to see the Air Officer Commanding (AOC) No. 1 Group Headquarters explaining my quandary. He dictated a message to my home station, which was sent with a degree of priority. In the message he stated that my services were being usefully employed with the assurance of me being on the first aircraft out of Torbay once the fog lifted enough for flying. Believing that my air force life might continue as before, my time was taken up with shift work and familiarizing myself with the sights of St. John's with Marjorie. Two days later the fog had not lifted so once more the AOC sent a second message with similar wording as the first one to my home station, once again emphasizing the fact that I would be on the first service aircraft departing for Moncton. Both messages were sent by me, personally. Surely that would do it.

It did not.

There were nearly 200 people waiting for a flight out once the fog lifted. My seat was assured when the first aircraft left Torbay Airport once the fog had lifted. (After the subsequent action had simmered down, I was nicknamed *Fog*.) The flight to Moncton did not take very long, but when we landed the service police were there waiting—I assumed—for me. Avoiding them was not difficult. A civilian bus was waiting to take passengers to the ferry; that was for me, so away we went. The service police had come in their own vehicle. They must have been told when the first flight from Newfoundland was due in Moncton.

My passing through the gate at 2ANS went without a problem; the guards did not recognize me. However, arriving in my barrack block my colleagues told me that big trouble awaited me. With that information the best thing was to surrender my identification card; open arrest was placed on me preventing me from leaving the air base. This was my 21st birthday. Two days later our chief instructor, a Canadian squadron leader who normally would have handled my case told me that Group Captain Hampton wanted to try my case personally. He asked me how the service police had been avoided at Moncton, when told the circumstances and no special tricks had been part of my return, he just chuckled, but he told me that the commanding officer had said that he would not tolerate interference from the RCAF, no matter what rank or position the defending officer might hold. So the next day my trial got under way.

August 4, 1944, two non-commissioned officers from my radio division as witnesses and a service policeman ushered me in before the group captain. The two messages from the Newfoundland AOC were visibly present on his desk. He asked me to give an account of myself. When my explanation of an authorized pass and the fact that I was on an air force station all those days as the two messages on his desk would verify he flew into a rage, tore up the messages saying if he heard one more word from me he would double my punishment, beside my being allegedly absent without leave (AWOL) was a more serious case with which he was tempted to charge me, it did not look good. He said, "I am going to make an example of you for the rest of you *colonists*." With that he sentenced me to fourteen days in the "digger" (military prison). One day was let off for good behaviour.

The activities involved during my cell days could do the Three Stooges credit. A service policeman would accompany me three times a day for meals; he would also escort me to church parade. I was the only miscreant, but both of us had to endure what the padre had prepared. At mealtimes in the mess hall, my colleagues would inform me of the goings on in the radio section. The padre thing lasted only one Sunday—because of my good behaviour, my release came before the next Sunday. During the daytime, my job was to clean the base of paper litter. Of course a police presence watched that the job was well done and that no one—there was just me, remember—made an attempt to escape. The padre sent a message to Marjorie stating that my release from prison would be August 17 and that she should meet me in Moncton on the following day; August 18, our original wedding date.

TWELVE

Married on Leave

The air force gave me thirty days leave, an accumulation of Newfoundland service leave as well as regular annual leave. Marjorie met me on the 18th, and we took the next train for Montréal. We stayed in Saint Lambert with Marjorie's Aunt Gwynne and her husband Major James Robertson. We bought wedding rings and had them engraved. Then on August 23, 1944, we were married in the Saint Lambert Presbyterian Church. My brother Jack was best man. He was on air force leave. We then travelled by train to Ottawa, staying in a hotel overnight.

Prior to enlisting in the RCAF, Marjorie was, at nineteen, the principal of a two-room high school in Cereal, Alberta. She had boarded with a newly arrived family from Ukraine. The father of that family was a section foreman for the Canadian Pacific Railway. This family had three young boys who, along with their parents, could not speak or read English. After hours, Marjorie would teach English with the assistance of newspapers and catalogues. Years later when she checked on what had become of the boys she was told one was a cabinet minister in the Alberta government, another was a medical doctor in Edmonton, and the third chap became a lawyer also in Edmonton. Marjorie enlisted in the air force when she was twenty-one.

The day after our wedding—the air force had given Marjorie and me travel warrants including meals on the train—we were on our way to meet each other's family; mine in Portage la Prairie, Manitoba, her parents in Edmonton, Alberta. We were received with pleasure from both sets of parents.

One incident that must not be left out was the Sunday we were in Portage. The young people of the church my parents attended arranged to have us honoured by the group in one of the homes. The planned activity was somewhat familiar to me, but Marjorie's background left her without a clue. Chairs were placed around the living room; Marjorie's chair was across the room from mine. Now we would see how well Eddie's bride knew the Bible. The idea was to quote a Bible verse when your turn came around. Poor Marjorie, when it came to her, all she could think of was a verse from the 23rd Psalm: "He makes me to lie down in green pastures." She did quite well; but then there was another round of more Bible verses. When it came to Marjorie, she hesitated a moment reaching through her minimal studies of theology but came out with, "I am the door," also quite biblical from John chapter 10. What she really meant was, "Show me the door!" No one had clued me in before hand, but it went off quite well—more than I could have expected. The next day we got on the train again heading for Edmonton.

Marjorie's parents were at the railway station, waiting for us. They were very proud of their daughter; her husband was accepted as a son of their own. We stayed with them for a week and then travelled to Banff for our honeymoon. We did the tourist things and the just-married activities too. The heavy-handed dealings meted out by the air force on me faded during our happy days together; the results of my meeting with the base commanding officer would come to trouble me and my career in the RCAF. I must include here an introduction to Marjorie's parents.

When I married Marjorie, I also inherited an interesting mother-in-law and father-in-law. While living in England Alfred C. Russell was a headmaster in a school in England. Violet Mason was a milliner who worked in a town hat shop. Alfred and his family arrived in Canada shortly after 1910. He was given a schoolteacher's position in Southern Alberta. After coming from Luton in England then settling down in Western Canada, the shock was huge, since they now lived in a teacher's house with two rooms. The floor was earth; the walls and roof were made of prairie sod.

During World War One, AC—as he preferred to be called—joined the Canadian army, went overseas as a lieutenant, and came back as a captain. The Alberta Ministry of Education offered him and other teachers who now were war veterans a location of choice where he would like to teach; he applied for a position in Edmonton where he started out in an elementary school as a teacher. Before long he was an assistant principal and ended his career as principal of Alex Taylor School in Edmonton. He was a gentleman of the old school, and I truly loved the man. When he died, Marjorie and I missed him so much that we decided to leave Edmonton and move to British Columbia, where I had been stationed earlier while with the Royal Canadian Air Force, and start a new life with our family.

While still in Edmonton and working for Alberta Government Telephones (AGT) I would take Marjorie's father with me on microwave site inspections. He was interested in my work. When he died, Marjorie and I purchased his house from his estate. If our move to

British Columbia had not materialized, we intended to move from our farm to his house. We rented it out, but the clients were not very punctual in paying their rent so eventually we sold it. With that we severed most of our ties to Edmonton.

Now Violet, Marjorie's mother, was a case of a different kind. She had a house built on Grierson Avenue in Edmonton. Actually she just drew the floor plans which were unique. While we were visiting with Marjorie's parents she asked if we would like to walk around a part of the city. I thought it a good idea since it was my first visit to Edmonton. While walking along Jasper Avenue we noticed a man, obviously one of the construction workers for a building under construction, scratching his derriere rather vigorously.

"Young man," Violet said, walking up to him, "are you going to a show?"

"Well no, why do you ask?"

"I just saw you picking your seat," she said.

I thought it best if we just disappeared before the man caught on. She often went, prior to our meeting, with Marjorie, to Premier Aberhart's evangelistic services at a camp near Wabamum Lake. She detested "high Anglican" services and priest dressed in skirts, as she described them. To make her point, she named her cat after a priest who came to see AC once in a while. Violet's cat was black and white but had a distinctly white strip of fur around its neck so she named it the same name as the Anglican divine who visited occasionally. She had a sharp wit, and did not tolerate humbug. I thought very highly of her, in fact I came near to loving her.

The return trip—Charlottetown for me and Newfoundland for Marjorie—was a preparation trip for how we would conduct our lives once the war was over. She had more holidays, so she stayed with me in Charlottetown for a week. She was restless to become a civilian again. Although she had a university degree and had left a high school principal's position to enlist in the RCAF, she was never offered a promotion. On the other hand, it was in the RCAF that we found each other, which made up for any occasion which might have made us more military-minded. In the fall of 1944, she asked to be released from the military, but it was my responsibility to claim her as my own—much like one might claim a chattel or possession. In October 1944 she joined me in Charlottetown.

A local farmer across the road from the air base had a two-room cabin on his property which we rented. The cabin was furnished, so we moved in. For Christmas dinner we invited one of my colleagues. Although Marjorie was rather worried about her lack of experience for such an event, it went off very well. On days off, Marjorie and I would go on long walks to Charlottetown and on the fishing docks. In our discussions, it was decided that I would go back to school and finish off my education to start a career.

One evening when on my ground stations turn, all the aircraft on my frequency channel were back from their training flight, so there was nothing to do but go home. The service fire engine roared by me but had to stop at the gate, so since the driver had to go by our place he waited for me to jump on the back. He did not stop at our driveway but kept on going for about half a mile, then turned abruptly through a ditch, through the barbed wire fence and headed for a clump of trees. We could see where one of our aircraft had crashed. The fireman needed my help to extricate the bodies from the aircraft. The plane, a Mark 5 Anson, constructed with plywood and canvas, had not exploded or caught fire. There were three sur-vivors including the radio operator, an associate of mine, who was walking around in circles with blood streaming down his face, for it had slammed into his radio equipment. Four people had died and were buried in the Charlottetown cemetery.

The war in Europe was near its end. There did not appear a need to train more air navigators, and the need for wireless operators also diminished. In May 1945 a posting came for me to the Northwest Staging route for onward posting to the Aleutian Islands. The assembly point for this operation was RCAF Station Edmonton, so we left our humble abode, got on the train, and headed west. The European enemy countries surrendered to the Allies while we were on the train heading west. Passing through the towns, villages, cities and countryside, we noticed the joy in the nation's population. If our stop was more than ten minutes, we would get off the train and participate in the celebrations. We stopped in at my parent's home for a day then on to Edmonton.

Edmonton's air force base was in a state of chaos. There were more able-bodied military personnel than the administration could handle. One day, while looking at the bulletin board, I noticed a memo which stated that those service personnel who had enough points could qualify for a discharge. Service in Canada was so many points while service overseas provided double the Canadian point value. Now, a fair amount of my service was in good old Newfoundland, which at that time was and had been a British colony, so next day my transfer to Winnipeg came through, and in two days my discharge papers also came along.

THIRTEEN

Return to Civilian Life

Veterans were given one hundred dollars as a clothing allowance. I bought a brown suit at Eaton's and also some everyday clothes. Marjorie and I looked for and found an upstairs suite for rent in Winnipeg. For me it was a matter of furthering my education, and within a few months my junior matriculation studies (Grade 11) graduation was complete. Then it was on to the University of Manitoba where a special class for veterans was being assembled; Grade 12 was first Year university. The curriculum was the same as the regular courses, but it was compressed. So "Johnny" had come marching home, but he found the academic environment very challenging and boring, resulting in his dropping out of the program well into his second year. The boring part was the instructors, who had been recruited from the pharmacy industry and came in for the pharmacy part of the curriculum. They were past middle-aged men who showed us how to count pills and the nitty-gritty of running a drug store. It was my career counsellor who had advised me to enrol in the pharmacy program; he had nothing to go on except that I had worked in a grocery store after school, and I did not really have an employment career in mind. If he had suggested engineering or even education, the program might have had better results. Another difficulty with which I had to deal every day was the long bus and street car commute from a Western Winnipeg suburb to Fort Garry in Southern Winnipeg, which took three hours of time every day.

In the meantime, Marjorie and I bought two lots in one of Winnipeg's suburbs, Kirkfield Park. We drew up plans for a house and dug a basement for 295 Parkdale Street. Lumber and other building materials were difficult to find. I had to be content to buy second hand rough lumber with which to cover the outside walls. There was old roofing paper stuck to the boards, so I had that side of the boards turned out, to be covered with stucco later on.

On April 30, 1946, our first child, Norma Louise, was born in the Grace Hospital in Winnipeg. This event became the interest of our neighbourhood. Some of my fellow former RCAF members, students at U of M, came to see Louise. They came in old cars and on motorcycles. I was the only student of the group who had a baby. Since Marjorie had also been in the RCAF she became an honoured member of the gang.

On June 25, 1947, Eric Edwin was born—a baby brother for Louise. We moved into our new house on his birthday. With a fair sized family to support, I had to decide what I should do—keep going to school with ninety dollars per month allowance from the federal government or try to find employment.

It became apparent that university schooling was not for me, so the need for employment became very important, but jobs were scarce, so to draw upon my air force experience a job was given me with Canadian Pacific Airline (CPAir) at the Winnipeg International Airport. I was placed in the stores department responsible for all the instruments and radio equipment for the Airline. Within a year the employees' union voted to strike for higher wages. Striking and its consequence were foreign to me; in fact union organizations were totally unfamiliar to me. However, union membership was a condition of employment, but not understanding the strike process left me wondering if I still worked for CPAir. The strike vote left much to be desired. We were all packed into a hall in Winnipeg where the vote was held—a secret by-ballot vote, when one of the leaders got up and stated, "We do not need a secret vote; all those in favour of striking stand up." Everyone stood up, so the strike was on without further discussion. The strike went on for several months.

In despair, we put our house, which we had just finished building, up for sale with a realtor and moved to Edmonton. CPAir was kind enough to ship our furniture and gave us train tickets for Edmonton. The manager also gave me a letter of introduction to the CPAir unit in Edmonton for a job as soon as the strike would be over. In the spring of 1948 the Airline closed the Winnipeg operation and moved everything to Vancouver

In Edmonton I built a cabin for the four of us on Marjorie's sister's spare lot. Before I could build the cabin, I needed to tear down their old barn and salvage the material for the cabin. In the meantime, my search for a job in the oil fields produced zero results; they needed skilled employees which left me out. Another major decision was made.

FOURTEEN

Johnny Goes Marching Again

In June 1948, with funds running low, there was no alternative but to re-enlist in the RCAF with my former seniority and qualifications intact. My work at RCAF Station Edmonton was tedious, but the authorities were looking for a placement for me. In the meantime, the air force administration suggested a six-month course in the Russian language might be helpful, so for six months a local college enrolled me in their after-hours program. Upon completion of the language course, I was offered a further course in the Russian language, in Texas. I had been in the RCAF for only six months, and I thought it better for me to decline the offer. In the meantime the RCAF bandmaster, Sgt Derek Stannard, asked me to join the air force station band as a trumpet player. Reading music was not my strong point. During practice sessions, the bandmaster would play the tunes a couple of times for me, and my memory did most of the rest. The band did about six public performances a year, but we had weekly practice sessions.

I must tell you of an incident in which I was involved. The RCAF head of telecommunications, a group captain, came to inspect the telecommunications set-up at our unit. Since I had just re-enlisted after a three year absence, the officer in charge put me in the storage room where the group captain would not likely look. Wrong. The good G/C came in and asked me about one of the spare items on a shelf.

"Young man," he said, "what is that equipment near where you are standing?"

Good grief, I had never looked at the equipment, but I saw the metal name plate, so peering at it I replied, "That sir is a Panadapter." (Whatever that meant)

"I commend you on your good eyesight," he said and with that he left to inspect other more interesting places.

The flight sergeant in charge of the telecom department taught me enough about amateur radio operations so that, although the Department of Transport exam was tough, the lessons learned stood me in good stead. When at Norman Wells my call sign VE8NW and certificate came through. My first transmitter was built in my spare time, and the receiver (radio) was a war surplus former aircraft radio the type that I had used when flying at Charlottetown. My posting came through to the Norman Wells, North West Territories Long Range Aid to Navigation (LORAN) unit in January, 1949. Marjorie, Louise, and Eric stayed in the cabin in Edmonton.

My work was with two other airmen and a flight sergeant, who was officer commanding the unit. We worked shift work around the clock with no days off. Our accommodation consisted of rooms in a semi-abandoned wartime barrack building with meals at the Canadian Imperial Oil's dining room. My duty period was from January to the end of October 1949. Communications with the outside world was by telegram through the Army Signals Corp. Of course there was general mail too. The RCAF had an aircraft had a weekly service flight schedule in and out. Our OC had a penchant for the bottle, so much so that, when he received his shipment of booze smuggled in—possession of liquor was forbidden—we might not see him for a week. In the summer of 1949 the air force sent in vehicles, and driver/mechanics, a novelty which soon wore off because the Norman Wells road was only a mile in length.

The Department of Transport (DoT) had a vacant furnished house by the airstrip. The resident-manager lived with the Imperial Oil crew, so he said the house was mine for the duration of my time at Norman Wells. I sent a telegram to Marjorie to pack enough clothing and other small items and to prepare to make the trip to Norman Wells. The air force service flight took me to Edmonton where Marjorie and our two children, Louise and Eric, were given permission to fly to Norman Wells with me; that was toward the end of June 1949.

Living up North would be a great experience for all of us. I was intrigued with the noise and violence of the ice breaking up on the MacKenzie River. One evening, as I was walking toward our LORAN building, I heard a dog team coming along the river. They were coming closer by the minute until they came into view. It was the local Roman Catholic priest coming back from a tour of his flock in Fort Norman and other villages along the way. I got to know Father Bernie Brown, formerly from Boston but now committed to Canada's North Country. He just loved the people with whom he made contact

The flight sergeant OC of the site was an American who had joined the RCAF during the war—but he still carried the US insignia on his uniform shoulders. He had disappeared for over a week when an air force aircraft landed with no one to meet whoever was on the plane but me. A well-known air commodore and his entourage de-planed, and the senior officer made a beeline towards me. After salutes were exchanged he demanded, "Where is the flight sergeant?"

My response was somewhat vague and suggested that he had not been seen that morning, which was true.

"I believe you have not seen him for a week, what do you say to that?" stated the air commodore.

My reply was in the affirmative. He told his aide to make a note of that. I invited the "sir" and his squadron leader aide to meet my family and have a coffee break. He agreed, but was curious about our accommodation. The two of us discussed the situation in Norman Wells. He asked Marjorie where she would like me to be posted once our tour was over. Since we had talked about that topic quite often she was able to reply, "To the Marine Squadron at Patricia Bay." Pat Bay was the RCAF version of heaven on earth. He told his aide to make a note of it; a message came about a month later that my next station was with 122 RCAF Marine Squadron, Patricia Bay. In the meantime he placed me in charge of the site since the flight sergeant was to be transferred to the wireless school at Clinton, Ontario. Good grief, I had no rank, only no-rank seniority! As an aside, while I attended a crypto course in Clinton several months later, the flight sergeant's and my paths crossed again, but this time he was being discharged after he had tried to commit suicide. He was a very sharp electronics technician, but the booze got the better of him.

The Norman Wells detachment was relatively undemanding. What became a problem was that the kitchen staff sold me groceries which we needed. The monthly expense was taken off my pay; that lasted until a squadron leader from Air Force Headquarters came up for an inspection tour noticed the sale of items to me. He called me to his office and read me the riot act, finishing with: "In the late '20s when I joined the air force, I was stationed in Northern Manitoba, my wife and I had to live off pork and beans and bannock; if that was good enough for us then, it is good enough now for you and your family."

With that he left. As soon as his aircraft was out of sight our old routine of buying groceries continued.

The walk from our house to the work site was a mile. One day some pipes sticking out of the ground caught my attention. One of the pipes had a valve with a handle near the top, so there was nothing else for it but to twist the valve "on." The result was a black stream of crude oil shot about twenty feet up in the air. Imperial Oil Limited (IOL) had several of these capped oil wells in the region.

Watching the IOL gardener, prepare a plot of land for a garden caught my attention since Norman Wells is set on permafrost soil. First he laid an extensive area with steam pipes; he covered them with about a foot of top soil brought in from the tree line. Later in the summer the garden was as good, or better, than the gardens down south. Although the soil at Norman Wells was permafrost just beneath the surface, the steam pipes, the rich soil, and long growing days meant that the vegetables almost leapt out of the ground.

My amateur radio was a great hobby for me although the technical part was difficult, especially that of building my own transmitter. It taught me many lessons and several hand-numbing shocks. My first contact was with a merchant ship in the Atlantic Ocean.

It came to pass that, as my term was coming to an end, the air force sent a young ex-aircrew flying officer to take over control of the site. The first thing he did, with my help, was to take an account of the inventory. Several tools and test equipment were missing; maybe they never were there. One of my colleagues in Edmonton wrote and told me that the new commanding officer accused me of taking them because mine was the only amateur radio station in Norman Wells. This upset me greatly since he had come into our house for coffee breaks and some meals as well and had depended upon me to show him the work routine and operation of the LORAN station. I had also shown him how my ham station worked.

When our family arrived in Edmonton, our boxes and suitcases were impounded and searched. Since none of the missing items were found we said goodbye to Marjorie's relatives, got on the train and ferry on our way to Patricia Bay, BC. The air force took care of shipping our goods including what we had left in our cabin six months earlier. We rented a motel until Emergency Married Quarters (EMQ) became available. The quarters consisted of previous wartime barracks which we could rearrange in any way to suit our needs. The rent, with everything supplied, was twenty dollars a month.

I bought our first car, a new British Ford Anglia, which cost $900. Marjorie learned to drive with that car; this was important because my job as radio operator on one of the High Speed Launches (HSL), the precursor of the present Canadian Coast Guard, meant being away from home for extended periods of time. My job was to operate the radio room and do maintenance on the equipment and on the ship's radar as needed, especially when away from home base. The radio operators also did shore duties at the home base when the boats were tied up. For several months it looked as though my ship adventures might come to an end; however, the navy medical officer gave me some seasick preventing pills. Until then the bobbing up and down of the HSL (these boats were wartime PT boats, now converted into search and rescue vessels) had made me very seasick. Once the pills were in my tunic pocket the type of sea or the swinging around of the boat never bothered me again.

Although many of our calls were people with boat troubles, one rescue trip will always remain with me. It was February 14, 1950 when a call came out at 0200 hrs; an American air force B36 aircraft, flying from Alaska to California, had one of its six engines on fire so the crew was ordered to bail out. The wireless operator on board had strapped his key down so that it sent out a steady note which one of my receivers on our HSL picked up for four hours before the plane must have plunged into the ocean. Where the crew abandoned their aircraft was along the coast a bit south of Prince Rupert. They had not worn winter clothes, so their survival depended on early rescue. HMCS Cayuga, a Canadian battleship, was the search master for all the people and boats involved. Every day our boat would rendezvous with the Cayuga, and my job was to establish our frequencies with theirs and agree to schedule times of the day to get in touch with each other. Our skipper arranged for rendezvous and rescue information. Stepping from our relatively small boat to the battle ship was like stepping onto an island; our boat would lift with the waves to arrive even with the big ship's deck, a moment when we, the skipper and I, would time it to step onto the ship's deck. My appointment was located in a lower deck where I found several of the sailors with barf buckets nearby. We did this routine every day for as long as I was there.

We had been there for several weeks. Marjorie's and my third baby was due on March 10, so somehow we had to get a replacement for me and food supplies for our crew. One day an American PBY

Catalina arrived with my replacement and groceries. My transfer to the American aircraft was routine, but the aircraft could not take off since the channel was not wide enough; the channel also had a dogleg in it, which prevented a long take off run. The pilot tried everything to take off in a normal way, but the circles made by the aircraft brought it closer to the shores. The flight engineer suggested Jet Assisted Take-Off (JATO) bottles which were then strapped to the fuselage; the next try shot us almost vertically towards the sky. By the way, the search parties rescued fourteen of the eighteen-man crew and passengers, but several family members of the lost passengers kept coming back for a few years to search for their loved ones.

We had flown for some time when I looked out and saw the Pacific Ocean on our left (port) side. That meant we were heading north rather than south. After several hours we landed in Kechikan, Alaska where we stayed for a few days and then headed for home. The pilot landed his aircraft at the Patricia Bay Airport, taxied it down a street near to our house, and let me out. With grateful salutes we then went our separate ways. Judith Patricia was born the next day, March 10, 1950. So with that, our family had expanded to three children.

It was at 122 Marine Squadron that the only promotion I was to receive was presented to me. In 1953 the Squadron disbanded. Some of the boats were turned over to the navy, others were sold, some airmen received promotions, others were given commissions, the majority were transferred to various air force units across Canada; my transfer was to Comox on Vancouver Island. My family now included five children. We rented a house in Courtenay.

Bob Shairp was a marine mechanic, transferred to Comox. He and I bought an army barrack block in Port Alberni and tore it down for the building materials. He and I stayed with friends of his in Port Alberni for a week and a half. Then we had all the lumber, timbers and even the bricks shipped to our building lots in Courtenay. I sketched a building plan for our house, which the Courtenay building inspector approved.

By the end of December 1954, we had built a house on the adjoining lot where we were living. The Comox air base had "sports day" every Thursday afternoon. Some of my colleagues would turn up on those days to help me build the house; some came with a six pack others with saws and hammers. They put the boards and shingles on the roof. Marjorie would have a pot of coffee and a stack of cookies ready for them. Both our nerves were on the brink at times when our "carpenters" were working near the edge of the roof.

My position at the air base was in charge of the telecommunications department, which included communications with the squadron's coastal patrols, and the cryptography unit.

In January 1955, a telegram came to me at the air base stating that Marjorie's mother had died, in Edmonton. The air force gave me leave to look after the "estate" so Marjorie could go to Edmonton for the funeral. She was also to see how her father was making out. When she returned, we decided to ask for a transfer to Edmonton or the nearby air base at Namao—just north of Edmonton—to help her father if help was needed.

Toward the end of January, the Comox RCAF curling team was flown to Edmonton and then to Cardston, Alberta, for bonspiels, then on back to Comox. I hitched a ride to Edmonton to find out how AC was making out. I stayed with him for a few days and then made my way to Penhold, where my brother Peter was stationed with the RCAF. Peter then drove me to Cardston, where I caught the curling plane back to Comox. After that Marjorie and I agreed that it would be in everyone's best interest if we, as a family, returned to Edmonton.

Within a week of our decision, a message came from Air Force Headquarters (AFHQ) in Ottawa, asking if Comox air base had someone with radio operator training and experience, as well as electrical technical abilities—right up my street—and who would be available for a six-month posting to Northern Quebec. After discussing with the Station Telecom Officer regarding what was on my mind about getting to Edmonton, he said he would endorse my application. The job was to set up a communications site with AFHQ and Air Transport Command near Montréal, at Great Whale River (GWR) in Northern Quebec. Those were days during the building of the Mid-Canada radar systems. My reply to the request was positive, with the provision that after my term at GWR, my transfer to Edmonton would be assured. The next message from AFHQ was to transfer me to GWR agreeing to my request.

My life has had some distraught moments; this was the worst up to that time. It was with a heavy heart that we said our fare-wells. Marjorie had to look after six children under ten years of age, sell the house, make arrangements for moving, and take care of utilities expenses. A local amateur radio operator in Comox teamed up a schedule with me; that and the mail were our only means of communication.

Upon landing in Quebec's Lachine Air Base, a truck was waiting to take me to a river where a float plane was waiting. There was just enough room for me because the rest of the space included a generator, radio equipment, some lumber, and a variety of tools, cables and an assortment of wire. Upon landing where the Great

J. Edwin Warkentin

Whale River empties into Hudson Bay, we were greeted by a group of Inuit people and the Canadian Government weather man. There were a few decrepit buildings left over from World War Two; it was up to me to decide where to "pitch my tent." One of the other buildings was a kitchen/dining room. The air force had brought in a few people preparing to lay the ground work for the new site. Some of the workers built a rudimentary radio shack, and so, with some assistance, my equipment was set up and running before long. There were other things of interest for me to explore such as the Hudson's Bay Post, the weather station, the Indian (whoops! First Nations) Chief, the Inuit Head Man (called a Deacon) and the Anglican Church representatives.

The gravel runway was also a relic from the war. Engineering companies, in recent times, found out that the sand was at least twenty-five feet deep, so the ground wire for my radio equipment was fastened to a large copper plate and immersed into the salt water of the bay. In six weeks, the chemicals had demolished the wire in the bay so this was replaced by larger gauge wire. Some of the Inuit (we still called them Eskimos in those days) were very good soap stone carvers; they gave me some of their craft works for my children.

One day in June, the inhabitants of the Inuit side of the village congregated on the shore of Hudson Bay watching a speck on the horizon approaching shore. One of my objectives while at GWR was to learn as much as possible about the people while living with them. Here, as it turned out, was an interesting spectacle in which, unwittingly, my standing in the community was being measured; after all, my position as the senior air force person on the site was fixed in peoples' minds. The speck came closer with the crowd cheering until the boat pulling a beluga whale hit the beach. Some of the men dragged the whale onto the beach where the head man (deacon) cut a cube of hide and meat from the whale's side and handed it to me with a wide grin and motioned for me to take a bite. To satisfy the crowd, with great effort, I put it into my mouth and my teeth dug into it. For one reason or another it tasted like walnuts. It slid down my throat easily enough, but the thought of repeating it caused a rebellion in my stomach, so the deacon took it and bit a mouthful before handing it to a member of his "cabinet." Having my curiosity satisfied for one day, duty called me back to my radio shack.

When the development contractor came with his entourage of engineers and clerks, one of the first buildings they started on was a control tower with three levels for my use. The second level became the radio room, and the third level was the control tower with windows all around it. An assistant meteorologist and an RCMP constable arrived. The policeman was a "ham" radio operator, but he had no equipment. We shared time on my apparatus. Three more radio operators also arrived to help with the radio traffic in the control tower. One of my responsibilities was operating the control tower for aircraft coming and going.

Work was continuing rapidly on the construction of the second runway. Many freighters came by water and had to be anchored out about a mile because the water was too shallow to come in further. The shipping agency had brought small barges, called lighters, with them for transferring their cargo to the shore. Cargo consisted of bulldozers, trucks, groceries, office furniture, bunk beds by the dozens and whatever else was needed. My first few days at GWR were rather carefree, but the volume of traffic and personnel that came through soon put a stop to that.

One day an air force pilot flying a Canso aircraft radioed in for permission to land and stay overnight. He had a whole village of Eskimos ill with tuberculosis on board. Evening was approaching, and the load still had a distance to travel to Moosonee, Ontario, so without a second thought, I suggested that the pilot park at the far end of the runway and have the passengers stay near the aircraft. When the aircraft arrived, the pilot, a squadron leader whom I had previously met, asked if food might be given to his passengers. This was no trouble, but on my way to the kitchen the police officer joined me to enquire about the aircraft that had just landed. When he heard the story he advised me to tell the pilot to load his passengers and shove off. Thinking that he might be in a better position to carry out his duties, I suggested that it was probably his duty to convey his opinion to the pilot; he took up the challenge. We wound our way back to the aircraft where the police officer said, after he had been introduced to the pilot, who himself was no one with whom to get into a tangle, "In the name of the Government of Canada and under the authority given me, I command you to get these passengers out of here before it gets dark." The pilot, flabbergasted at the audacious manner of a young constable said, "And under the authority I have given myself, you can bloody well salute me and (do something to yourself which would be very inconvenient)." The police officer did the former, but the latter was out of my sphere of interest. Some of the crew members were posted as security to keep the GWR Eskimos away from the newly arrived infected passengers. Meals arrived, the passengers slept under the aircraft's wings and left early the next morning after breakfast had been provided.

Some time later Air Marshal John Plant came in for an inspection—actually to visit his son, a university student working for the summer with the contractor. During our discussion about the activities at GVR, the discussion came around the aircraft staying overnight at the end of the runway. He asked me who the pilot was, when I told him he roared with laughter saying that was what he would have expected. We drank coffee, more than normal because once the air marshal got going the yarns flew by very quickly and often. He asked me about my activities and he wanted an introduction to the Anglican couple and their "take" on GWR. Sid Wilkinson and his wife Norma, a nurse, had been recruited in England by the Anglican Church in Canada, one had been a former Salvation Army officer, and the other had a Pentecostal church background prior to coming to Canada.

Some of the native women upon finding out that Norma Wilkinson was a nurse would make unnecessary calls, mostly for her company, but it was beginning to get out of hand. Upon dropping in on the Wilkinson's house one day it came to my attention that there were four native ladies waiting their turn. Sid lost his patience momentarily and asked one of the patients to pull down her trousers for him to apply an injection; she did as she was told, not a pretty sight, Sid whammed the needle into her rump which was accompanied by a gasp. All four "patients" beat a hasty retreat; word got around.

On another occasion an Eskimo girl of about sixteen years of age had become pregnant. By now GWR had a large complement of air force and construction personnel. It was obvious—to the investigators in Ottawa at least—that one of our air force men must be guilty; the investigators arrived from Ottawa. Prior to the investigators' arrival, I received a message to not let any of the air force personnel leave the site. They wanted to question each air force person to find which one was guilty. I was rather upset by the conjecture of these legal inspectors. Using what little authority which had been granted me, this process was rejected. My suggestion was for them to look at some of the civilian workers or, perhaps one of the Hudson's Bay staff. One of their staff had recently been transferred to a position in Labrador. It was useless asking the girl; she just giggled and seemed to enjoy the attention. The young man was brought in from Labrador, admitted guilt and readily agreed to support the child once it was born, adding that he wanted to marry the girl. The last chapter was not concluded during my remaining time at GWR.

Toward the end of October my new posting from Air Transport Command (ATC) came in; it was to Dorval, just out of Montreal. My shock had no limits. After letting my steam subside I wrote a message and sent it to ATC reminding the powers that a posting to Dorval was not part of our agreement since my departure from GWR was to be to Edmonton. A further bit of information for them to consider was that my rank had been greatly imposed upon so now the promises given me earlier in the year should be respected. Two days later the personal aircraft of the Air Officer Commanding, an air-vice marshal, arrived with the AOC himself on board. Upon meeting the aircraft he asked to see the OC in charge.

"I am he," I said. "May I help you?"

"I have come here to see what kind of person we sent up here," he said. "You know, young man, you came pretty close to insubordination."

There was no point in having a debate, so after a cup of coffee, we toured the site. I introduced him to the superintendent who showed what still had to be done. Before leaving the next day, he offered me a ride to Trenton with a voucher for a return trip by civilian plane on my way back. I accepted his invite. A kind fellow service man gave me a ride to Toronto where one of my brothers was living. After four or five days, my brother gave me a ride to Trenton where a seat was available to GWR. A week later, after returning to GWR, my transfer to the air base at Namao (Edmonton) came through; it was to take place in two weeks.

Now my days at GWR were numbered. There were quite a few important (to me) people to see before leaving. The RCMP chap bought my radio equipment. The head of the Indian tribe and the head of the Eskimo community had become friends of mine, so it was important that we said our adieus. Of course the Anglican Wilkinsons had become close friends, so we spent some time together. Again, just as an aside, Sid posted notices around the camp that three evenings would be services for the Eskimos, three would be for the Cree Indians, and one would be for the Anglican worshippers although "nonconformist" people would be welcome. I was, perhaps, the most nonconformist on that site or any site for that matter, I told him not to use a term like that in Canada.

Sid joined me to visit the Eskimos and the Cree Chief. Sid always carried his Bible and an Eaton's catalogue. Several Eskimos had jobs with the general contractor, but they had no bank so Sid would make up an order for blankets, clothing for winter wear, camp stoves, canvas to wind proof their tents, rifles and ammunition. The Hudson's Bay store tried to put a stop to his secular activities, but nothing came of it.

In my absence, Marjorie had sold the house, paid off our utilities, and bought winter clothes for the children—after all we were going to Edmonton. It was now nearing the end of November. Prior to my leaving Courtenay for GWR, I had bought a British Ford

J. Edwin Warkentin

Estate Wagon; it was a small station wagon with enough seats for our family; actually all the seats except the two in the front folded into the floor of the flivver, resulting in a fairly large truck space. When all loose ends had been tidied up, we started out for Nanaimo where we caught the ferry to Vancouver. About half way to the ferry our car's small engine blew a head gasket, but the driver (me) blew a larger head gasket. We limped on to the ferry like a tiny steam engine just as it was getting ready to leave. Once in Vancouver we stayed with my parents for the night. I took the vehicle to the freight shed for onward shipping to Edmonton and had my father take us to the railway station. All eight of us breathed a great sigh of relief once we were seated. The Grey Cup football game had been played in Vancouver the previous day so there was a rowdy crowd on board the train headed for Edmonton.

Upon our arrival in Edmonton, we looked and found a motel that could accommodate our family. It was the end of November and temperature outside was − 20°F, which is *very* cold. On my way back from Great Whale River, with AC's help, we found a house for sale and bought it in the north east part of Edmonton. In the meantime, we had settled down in the motel, where we stayed for three weeks until our belongings arrived. Our little Ford came, but had to be towed to a service station where a head gasket repair was done and a dip stick heater was installed; there was nowhere that a block heater could be fitted on to the engine. The movers arrived with our furniture and housewares, so by the end of Christmas holidays 1955 our school-aged children were pretty well established.

My duties as NCO in charge of the radio room and the crypto room were not very demanding, not after my time at Great Whale River. The Station Telecom Officer (STelO) suggested I apply for a commission as a flying control officer—that was in January 1956. He recommended the application, and the commanding officer, after an extensive interview, gave me a high recommendation. It passed through North West Air Command (NWAC) where it was also recommended, but when my application reached AFHQ it was turned down because of my past record at Charlottetown in 1944 without so much as a look at my present experience and record.

During one of the disturbances in the Middle East in 1956, an aircraft squadron was being assembled in Calgary for onward operations to the hot spot. My project was to take charge of the communications systems, but Middle East tempers calmed down, and the squadron was disbanded with me going back to Edmonton.

In April 1958, the usual annual promotion list came through with my name on the list for promotion. Later that week a posting came through for me to 5 Radio Unit in Whitehorse. Upon my return from GWR, I made a promise to Marjorie that I would never put her in that position again. So when the Whitehorse posting came through, accompanied with the information that there were no houses available either on the air base or in the town itself, I requested it be cancelled since I had already served at two northern sites, one as officer commanding, a position way beyond what my rank should permit; with months away from my family. All this coincided with me having to sign up again since my two five-year terms were completed. I was told that my concerns were of no interest to the RCAF. An impasse took place, I would not sign up under the conditions presented, so my pending promotion was cancelled, my posting was cancelled and I was ordered to leave the base with my family within the month.

(Recently, for the past eight years, a lawyer and former army colonel, has tried to get the Charlottetown incident expunged from my records; for several reasons: first, the Long Service Medal denied me; second, no service pension; third, my recommended commission forfeited. The lattermost consideration has been lost without possible recovery, but the first two might still be achieved—but so far the military personnel who could bring it to pass have been dragging their feet. It is now 2013 and the initial response from the decision maker has been negative, but the former colonel lawyer is determined to continue with it.)

FIFTEEN

Adjusting to Civilian Life

Prior to leaving the air force, the only engineering business I had applied for a job, was with Alberta Government Telephones (AGT) as an assistant microwave engineer. What got me the job was the course in Radar, which I had taken by correspondence from Radio College of Canada, while up North.

The technologies of the two systems, radar and microwave communications have similarities; they both use waveguides rather than wire for attaching the transmitter/receiver to the antennas which also have similarities in design. I was given a new station wagon full of test equipment the likes of which I had never seen. My initial job was to go along with an engineer from Motorola, the company which had supplied much of the communications equipment. Upon completion of system tests, I would accept them on behalf of AGT.

Several tough times lay ahead. One was the fact I now wore civilian clothes rather than military garb, and I had no one to turn to for assistance, although that had seldom been available during my air force years in any case. The new equipment had manuals over which I burned the midnight oil, so to speak. I was alone with the Motorola engineer for much of my first year; I could not very well let him know that some of the techniques and descriptions were totally foreign to me. He did accept me at par with himself. At the end of my first year the "assistant" portion was dropped from my title. When the systems were up and running, it was my job to go to the remote sites, ten in all, to do tests and fine tune the equipment. I was able to return home nearly every evening although there were times when I had to stay for a day or two in a country fleabag hotel.

The self-dependency which I had developed and under which I had operated while with the RCAF at Great Whale River came into play now; for example, there was a time when the whole telecommunications systems from Edmonton to northern Alberta failed. The trouble was pinpointed to be between Edmonton and Sangudo, the second repeater in the chain. I travelled to Sangudo, 90 miles by road, tuned up the transmitters and receivers to peak performance, then to Onoway, the half-way site back, a distance of 60 miles. No signal was coming from Edmonton so obviously the problem had to be there, even though their equipment was optimally tuned.

At the Edmonton site, the general manager of AGT along with the government cabinet minister responsible for AGT were pacing back and forth, reminding me that they were losing thousands of dollars in revenue, and that their constituents in the North demanded action to have their telephone system restored. To get away from this harangue, I went back to Onoway. By now it was early evening, and I was exhausted. Driving into the site I looked up at the antenna 200 feet up, more for inspiration than problem solving. Then I saw it. The ten foot antenna dish was tilted toward the ground. On going over to the tower I noticed a neat pile of bolts, nuts and washers. The lower bracket of the antenna had shaken loose in the wind and the upper bracket operated like a hinge, allowing the antenna to tilt.

With the hardware in my pocket, I climbed the tower. The towers were large enough to climb up inside. Once I was at the antenna height I had to manoeuvre to the outside of the tower, hang on with one arm, move the antenna out with my feet, and then slip the bolts back into the bottom bracket. To say the least, it was nerve-wracking, but it worked, and before long everyone was communicating once again; after that, AGT established a tower maintenance policy for the entire province.

On a Sunday night in January, I was called out to the Drayton Valley site (a distance of 100 miles) to restart the microwave system which had failed. On this occasion, the roads were very icy and the ditches were level with the roads with snow. A fox ran across the road, and in order to avoid hitting it, I slid into the ditch. It was Sunday midnight, miles from the nearest house. The doors of my station wagon were held shut by the depth of the snow; I did not have a two-way radio. I crawled out of the door window. Within an hour a large garbage truck appeared, hooked his chain to my vehicle and pulled me out. It was not long after, that AGT stationed a technician at the site.

Drayton Valley was just coming into its own as an oil-producing region. Exploration by various oil companies showed positive results. The tests were constantly being relayed to their laboratories in Edmonton, Calgary, and Toronto by microwave radio systems. Several times I saw spies on telephone poles with high-powered binoculars trying to read the drill cores of their competitors. These cores were four inches in diameter and ran for up to twenty feet in length.

On another occasion I was sent to explore the radio site in the Peace River district for a future microwave location. The local radio technician took me to inspect one of the remote mobile radio sites.

Again, it was winter with much snow. While driving along on a narrow snow-ploughed trail we suddenly heard a loud horn blast coming from somewhere. The radio technician wrenched his wheel to one side and we drove through the ditch into the bush. I thought the guy had been up north too long. We were stranded. Before long a huge oil tanker truck flew by; it was its horn we had heard. He stopped, hooked his cable on to our truck and pulled us out. You see, the road had only one track and he was bigger than we were.

The experiences acquired while with AGT stood me in good stead for future employment. For much of my time with AGT, I had to fly by the seat of my pants, so to speak, but with much reading and experimenting, I caught on to the various radio systems. The fact that there is no one there to assist creates dismay, shock, innovation, adventure and self-confidence, in order to take control when you know you can't give up.

Alberta Government Telephones had a microwave radio system heading west from Edmonton to Edson, not far from Jasper. A repeater site was located at Wildwood just off Highway 16. I would go there for regular monthly maintenance inspections. The building and antenna tower were located in a farmer's field inhabited by a fierce bull—this is not to be taken as an *ordinary* bull story. To get into the site, I had to open the ten foot wide gate made of three strands of barbed wire with a pole at one end, looped to the next fence post. This day I did not see the bull so I opened the gate, drove the station wagon through, got out and closed the gate; still no bull. Once I was in the building I left the door open. In the meantime while I was doing the routine inspection I heard a snort outside and then the beast tried come in through the open doorway to get at me; he got stuck. With a series of deafening roars and spit flying in all directions he could not get in or out for fifteen minutes. By now I was getting anxious so I punched him rather violently in the nose with more spit flying—his spit—actually the bull was firing from both ends as I found out once he left. Eventually he got out with my help. To vent his fury he attacked my car, denting it by pushing it around. When he wandered out of sight, I ran for the car drove to the gate and there he was. The standoff lasted for about an hour when he just wandered away I opened the gate and escaped.

When I was transferred to the main maintenance centre in Edmonton, one of my responsibilities was to set up closed circuit television systems to and from various locations in the Edmonton area. One such event was after the Manning government had won one of its many provincial elections. The opposition party was reduced to four members. Our microwave engineering department was asked to set up a closed circuit link to the local CBC station for televising the opening of the legislature. In order to make certain one of the cameras would be trained on the opposition party's seats, I asked Premier Manning where the four members would be located. He said, "I had thought of bringing in a telephone booth for them; what do you think?" I thought that would be a good plan since the door could be closed if they became too unruly.

Another television pickup was from the University Hospital to the MacDonald Hotel where a medical convention was underway. We got the link hooked up with the camera installed in the operating room for some close-up video shots. Two scheduled operations had to do with some rather delicate parts of women's plumbing.

Later on another video shoot was a closed circuit television heavy weight fight between Sonny Liston and a challenger whose name escapes me. It was televised from Madison Square Gardens in

New York, across the United States to Seattle, up to Vancouver and on to Edmonton where the televised display would terminate in Edmonton Gardens. The promoter of this event was a former heavy weight wrestler, a veritable giant. The television image was projected on to a large screen: the arena was packed out. The usual preliminary bouts came across fine as far as the picture was concerned. Just before the main event was to come in the signal went dead. We found out later that the repeater site in Bellingham, Washington had burned down. The promoter was in a rage—a *giant* rage. He paced up and down beseeching, "Holy Mary, Mother of God, please help me!" Mary was either not listening or too busy with other things than to come to his rescue. He then looked around for a target and spotted me. He picked me up by the scruff of the neck, lifting me in line with his face and asked, with a series of expletives, how soon was I going to have it fixed, otherwise he had some rather unsavoury plans for me. When my feet hit the ground they just kept going. The next day's newspaper gave an account of the trouble, stating that the promoter had "lost his shirt."

In the autumn season for four years running, I would go on hunting trips with four experienced Nimrods. The Eaton's in Edmonton had Lee-Enfield wartime rifles for sale, so in preparation of the first onslaught, I bought one and a box of bullets. The first trip into the wilds of Alberta came about when friends of ours came to visit from the Grand Prairie region. Jim had brought a neighbour along to add experience to our hunt. It was evening when we arrived at our "command centre" where we pitched our tent. To reconnoitre the area, the three of us took separate trails through the bush. By the time I turned around to go back it was almost dark. Of course I had taken my rifle, just in case. I heard an animal stomp through the underbrush towards me. I hid in some bushes just off the trail with rifle on the ready; the animal stopped, I could see it was black, so thinking it was a bear, I raised my rifle and was ready to fire when the animal let out a low *Moo*—it was a local farmer's cow. Next morning after coffee, the three of us went in three different directions. I hid myself behind some bushes when I heard what I thought was a moose stomp through the bushes coming towards me. Once again I cocked the rifle when Andre, Jim's friend, appeared. He had wandered off his direction of hunting, and little did he know how close he came to the wrong end of a rifle.

The other expeditions did not come off any better, although on one trip, while I was resting on a log, eight elk passed by, and as I was not prepared to shoot anything, the grand parade, those animals looked royally striking as they passed along unawares that I was nearby. I just enjoyed being outdoors in the fall season taking pleasure in the beautiful countryside.

Before leaving the air force we bought a house on 139th Street in Edmonton. Two reasons for the location were that it was within easy walking distance to school for the children and it would assist in establishing a Southern Baptist church nearby.

I had to build extra rooms in the basement of our house and also a garage because winter's arrival was inevitable. We lived in the house for two years, until we purchased five acres just north of Edmonton on what is now 82nd Street, Steel Heights, in 1960. In my travels on AGT business, I kept my eyes open for such a place. The purchase price for five acres, a house, barn and double garage was $19,000. Veterans Affairs Canada gave us a loan of $5,000—actually this was part of Marjorie's rehab grant from her air force days—to be repaid upon the sale of the property. If we kept the property for ten years the loan would be forgiven; of course it was not forgiven because we moved to Victoria five years later. The farm life was a great experience for our family. One of the priorities was to buy a horse, preferably a riding horse; within a year we had two horses, the colt came without me knowing it was on its way. Close in priority was a cow for milk—a Jersey cow. She presented us with a calf a few months later. Then we had to have chickens and a dozen turkey chicks. To round off our zoo, we bought two piglets. The older children were given chores to look after the critters. Even now, although over forty years have passed, my children still enjoy reminiscing about those days.

SIXTEEN

Old Time Religion

We must go back for a moment to the mid–1800s after my great-grandparents with their family had established themselves in a Russian-style community in Canada—the type of settlement which would make sure that the new immigrants would have social surroundings and make certain that they would stick together in this new land. Farms were allocated to each family. The fabric that bound them together was their belief in God and their commitment to their Christian heritage. A number of these settlements were administered by a council of men headed up by an elder who was also the spiritual leader of the community. My great-grandparents, after having a look around their settlement, realized that there was much fertile land surrounding their neighbourhood, which could be obtained under an agreement from the government for little or no cost. When patriarch Warkentin asked permission to leave the Mennonite settlement to establish an independent farm for himself and his family, he was turned down with a warning that, if he did go, his family in that day and in future years would be shunned by the remaining residents of the community and their descendents. It also meant that people from the family who died could not be buried in the churchyard cemetery. With the "bit between his teeth" the patriarch moved his family to establish a homestead at Haskett not very far from the American border. There was another more practical reason to move away from the Mennonite community, and that was to integrate into the English speaking quarter. Reflecting on what his forefathers had been through to escape ecclesiastical intrusion into family matters as well as spiritual interests, patriarch Warkentin and subsequently grandfather Warkentin would have nothing to do with religious activities, an attitude which was passed down to his children and some of his grandchildren, of which I am one.

In my youth, our family attended an evangelical—maintaining the doctrine of salvation by faith—church in Morden, Manitoba. My recollections involve Sunday school attendance; this was during the great depression. I could not understand the stories because I did not understand English at that time. The teacher called the roll, and the children would respond with *present*. Now *present* was perhaps the first English word I learned, and it had the connotation of a gift because when grandfather visited us he would bring, in his own words, a *present*. That was the disappointing part of Sunday school attendance—no presents. On the other hand, once we moved into town from a depressing life on the farm, my father and two of my brothers became violinists in the church orchestra, I became a church orchestra member too, playing a banjo.

My father had fall-outs with young preachers from time to time. Most of these events occurred when the reverend refused to participate in some of the manual work that needed doing around the church building. On one such occasion father suggested that we, that is children, go to the local Baptist church. I was sixteen at the time, an age when cheeky children begin to question almost everything.

The Baptist church services, to me, seemed to be more worship minded than what we previously had experienced. This attitude of mine would come back to bite me before too long. When I enlisted in the air force during the war, my dog tags listed me as BAP; I must have told them what my leanings were.

Marjorie and I made a commitment to God in 1950, although I had made an earlier commitment in my youth when a local preacher asked "are you ready to meet Christ who is liable to return at any moment?" Well, as we all know, the second coming to sweep God's people up to glory has not arrived. Marjorie had been brought up a nominal Anglican with not much theological training, so this experience was very important to her. We were baptized in a country church near Victoria, BC, in 1950. On my short wave radio we picked up radio station HCJB, Quito, Ecuador, once in a while. It was and still is a Christian radio station. We were both intrigued and interested in their programs, so much so that we made enquiries for becoming staff members. Marjorie, since she had practical teaching experience, would teach school age children, and I would be on the radio engineering staff. Their North American contact was Moody Bible Institute in Chicago, IL. We filled out the necessary forms, with the provision that we had to do certain requirements before we would me accepted. I had to memorize 125 Bible verses and Marjorie had to take a comprehensive course on the first five books of the Bible, the Pentateuch. We did all of that, completed our application; I had to request a leave of absence from the air force, which I did. Then we were told that we had too many children—three, which they had known right from the time we had made enquiries, so we would not qualify. The commanding officer of 122 Squadron had not submitted my request, but had it lying on his desk, "in case I came back," to quote him. I asked if he would return it to me, which he did. Those turns of events made me pause and start my questioning the philosophy of overseas missions, which is still a question in my mind, as well as some of the other doctrines to which I had subscribed. Up until this occurrence I had, mentally, immersed myself in the Baptist (no pun intended) rituals. I lost all interest in ever trying such a career again.

In the autumn of 1953, after I was transferred to RCAF Station Comox also on Vancouver Island, we built a house in neighbouring Courtenay, and since there was no Baptist church in the community, I felt it was our duty to help get one established. By now we had five children which I thought was a nucleus for a congregation, although there were several other displaced Baptist people who joined with us. The group became the Courtenay Fellowship Baptist Church. We rented a hall owned by the Eagles Club for Sunday services. I became the Sunday school superintendent (more like novice) and Marjorie was the pianist. This carried on for a bit longer than a year. A student from the Baptist theological college in Vancouver came on weekends to conduct the Christian services. In about a year after that arrangement, he graduated, married and brought his wife over to live with him and help him. He was now the full time pastor. It did not take him long to remove Marjorie from the piano bench and have his bride take over. His wife was a good pianist, but the replacement process might have been done a bit more tactfully.

In November 1955, just after I got back from Great Whale River, I was posted to Edmonton. We lived in a motel for nearly four weeks waiting for our goods to arrive from Courtenay. I had purchased a house in the city. We attended a Baptist church just off Kingsway; there were now eight of us so it meant that we filled a whole row of seats. The fifth Sunday we were welcomed as new visitors. I was not impressed with their emphasis with regard to attention paid to visiting university professors and political dignitaries who would be invited to sit on the platform for all to see.

I had heard of the Canadian Southern Baptist Churches, so we thought we would give one of them a try—*when will I ever learn?* Well, we did give it a try, for five years. I have since recovered from the hectic lifestyle, busy, busy, busy! On Fridays evenings I checked my air force uniform and brains into the clothes closet until Monday morning. Saturday was usually scheduled for the men of the church to do some physical work after hearing a pep talk by the preacher. We could usually have Saturday evenings with our family, although mother made sure that all the clothes were clean and pressed; father made sure all the shoes were polished. Sunday, in reflection was insane; Sunday school in the morning followed by morning worship church service, afternoon was Bible study, early evening was Training Union (Southern Baptist indoctrination) followed by the evening service. I usually breathed a sigh of relief Monday morning. One of the works of the Southern Baptist church very much in its favour was that if the mother of a family was ill, no matter how long, the rest of the membership would sign up to deliver a hot dinner every evening. In the fall of 1957, our family—except one of the boys— came down with Mumps; every evening at dinner time a dinner complete with dessert would be waiting on the doorstep. This kept up until our quarantine was lifted. Many churches could take a lesson from that.

We made the break by moving to our acreage. Then, as if I had learned nothing, I thought we might have another go at the previous church, since that church had, in the meantime, acquired a new "divine" who ran a tight ship. He and his wife had several children who were of high school age.

One day while out of town on my microwave inspection tour, one of the technicians came with me. After we had eaten our lunch at the local fleabag hotel, we noticed some activity which I thought looked like a fight in a car parked a bit out of the parking lot; I thought I recognized the car, so we went over to investigate. What was going on was one of the preacher's children getting it on with a female church member. On my way back into town, I stopped off at the church and informed the preacher about what my colleague and I had witnessed. He was furious, telling me to mind my own business and suggesting that I had made a mistake—I had not. He went on to threaten that, if I did not retract my statement, he would set about to ruin me. He nearly did, for example one day after leaving for an out of town job I returned home to pick up an equipment manual I had been studying. There was the preacher's car in my yard. I went into the house, and upon seeing me, he left in a hurry. I learned that he had been there several times when I was up country on maintenance inspections. Marjorie told me that his main theme was, "are you sure that you know what your husband is up to when he is out of town?"

He was so convincing that Marjorie had burned her wedding dress. He had told her that on one occasion he said that he had followed me and had seen another person in my company car with me and that person looked like a woman. It could well be that he had seen a trainee technician with me because I would take junior technicians with me; we did not have any women in the engineering department, or that he had fabricated the stories to fuel the threat he had imposed on me. It took Marjorie and me some time to get over the ordeal; in fact that was one of the reasons for us to pack up and move to Victoria. It also made Marjorie determined to study the biblical first languages to understand how preachers who had, in most cases, studied the Scriptures could have such evil dispositions. From these research projects on her part came her Master of Theology thesis, *Ordination,* a subject over which we had many discussions, and up to that time, my experiences with our denomination, gave me an opportunity to read Marjorie's book and be satisfied that my doubts were confirmed.

While I am on the topic, let me tell you of some of my wife's experiences in her studies at the local Baptist college and seminary. Marjorie took a basic course in Koine Greek, the language of the New Testament. This was at a time when all seven of our children had departed the nest. While the children were still at home, she felt responsible for them; they and I honour her for that.

Marjorie and I had seven children.

Louise was born in Winnipeg in April of 1946, while I was attending the University of Manitoba. She is married and has four children and seven grand-children. Louise was perhaps the most acquiescent of the lot, but she had a mind of her own. Louise became efficient playing the piano.

Eric too was born in Winnipeg while I was at the University of Manitoba—in June 1947. He is married and has three children and seven grandchildren. He has always had an independent streak in him. In his early years, whenever I gave him a chore, he would round up his buddies and stand over them to make sure the work by them was done properly. He also played hooky several times while in grade one.

Judith was born in Victoria's Royal Jubilee Hospital in March of 1950. She lives on Vancouver Island with her husband. She had two children—her son Joseph died recently—and has five grandchildren. She and I bonded very early in her life. I was assigned to the after-midnight bottle feeding shift. I would put a glass bottle with baby formula on the stove in a pan of water. Then I would hold her in my arms while attempting to do some amateur radio contacts. We both would fall asleep and be awakened by a terrible crack when the pan and bottle had boiled dry. This happened several times. She learned to play her violin.

Peter was also born in the Royal Jubilee Hospital, in January of 1952. He is married and has five children—two of whom were adopted from Haiti—and two grandchildren. As a child he never crawled, but one day he stood up and walked before he was one year old. He was a thinker. I would take him to my air force work once in a while and turn him over to a couple of airwomen who just adored him, making me promise to bring him back the following week. He has become a successful business entrepreneur.

Andrew was born in the Seventh Day Adventist Hospital in Sidney on Vancouver Island in December of 1952. He is married and has four daughters, and six grandchildren. He was not well, physically, for the first year of his life; he could not digest cow's milk, so it was some time after the introduction of goat's milk that he rallied. We got a lot of satisfaction watching him develop not only physically but also mentally. He always wanted to know how mechanical and electrical things worked. Andrew has recently retired from a high school teaching position.

Paul was born at the Saint Joseph's Hospital in Comox on Vancouver Island in October of 1954. He is married, and has two children. Paul was perhaps the most looked after baby in our family. When I went to Great Whale River, Quebec for the better part of 1955, Marjorie often wrote about Paul's progress. Some of his siblings thought he was spoiled, but his mother just doted on him. She wrote to me saying that Paul would scold his bottle when it was empty.

Edward was born in Edmonton's Royal Alexandra Hospital in January of 1958—the same hospital as his mother thirty-seven years earlier. He is married and has three children. His eldest daughter lives in Australia. Edward was born just a few days late to start school at his approaching age—six years. His mother taught him at home for grade one. He made such good progress that he spent just half days doing his lessons. His mother wrote to me, when she was visiting her aunt in South Africa, asking me to not pay any attention to Ted's lobbying for a new bicycle—he did not need a new one. He grew up with the computer age.

All in all Marjorie and I enjoyed having a large family. The dining table had to be enlarged to accommodate everyone. I have regretted the times I was away from home on air force work while the children were growing up. Their mother kept me up to date with the family goings on. She had the major part in their upbringing and did a good job of it.

Judith, Peter, Andrew, Paul, and Edward were all born while I was a member of the Royal Canadian Air Force. We were transferred to various stations within Canada, which meant that their school years were interrupted several times. In fact, during the ten years in peace time that I was with the air force, we moved six times. I retired from the air force when I was posted to Whitehorse. Their mother and I marvelled at the fact that none are alike but most have some positive characteristics of their mother—thank goodness. We often talked about their progress in school and wondered, at times, with some concern, which career path they would take. In the final analysis they seemed to know what they wanted to do, and each one has shown an independent career spirit.

Once the language study bug had bitten there was no holding Marjorie back. In the courses she took at the seminary, her main interest was in learning Hebrew and Greek. Eventually she could read the books of the Bible in their original languages. Mind you, she had to take the regular theological curriculum as well. She also developed a correspondence course in Koine Greek for people who were interested and yet too far away to attend a theological college. After she had received her Bachelor of Theology degree, she continued her studies and attained her Master of Theology degree. The MTh required a thesis for completion. The theological degrees were recognized by the University of British Columbia through an act by the Government of British Columbia. When she started the seminary courses, the professor teaching one of the theological courses saw her seated in the classroom and said that he would not start the course until *that woman leaves*. He said, "I teach church pastors, and women do not fit the plan." Since she was not about to leave, he went to complain to the seminary president, who previously had given her his approval.

When I reflect back on her church-induced problems and our mutual discussions regarding the church ministries and the attitude of some of the seminary professors, it's no wonder that Marjorie and I thought the subject of her thesis should be *Ordination*. She had researched the subject and discovered that no denomination had ever thought of looking into ordination beginnings or how it prospered. The seminary committee that validated her thesis subject told her it was a suitable topic. When it came to defending it before the faculty committee, she failed to pass; one of the criticisms was that she was challenging one of the tenets of the church. It seems to me that *many* of the beliefs presented from the pulpit could bear looking into. I happened to be in Ontario on education business at that time but hurried home.

The chancellor of the seminary decided Marjorie should apply the following year with an outside adjudicator being present. It happened, and she passed. She had been an adjunct member of the faculty until then, but there came a parting of the ways. She had come to the conclusion that the faculty were no more reverend than anyone else; after all, *"holy and reverend is His name."* Psalm 111:9. An outcome was that the entire episode came to the attention of Eerdmans Publishing Company, and they sent one of their editors to Vancouver and asked Marjorie to put the thesis in book form. It took her a year, but she won a contract to have it published. Her book sold quite well the first year under the sponsorship of Eerdmans, which genuinely pleased her.

Marjorie did not live long enough to receive the full benefits of her endeavours. She had lined up several other topics worthy of research and production such as missions, tithing, prayer, church services and its leaders, the residence of the soul after death, among others. She felt there was a great lack of information available for church members and students. With today's computers and internet she would have been in her glory; however, in January 1984 she suffered a massive heart attack and died. I miss her challenging mind, which often came to my rescue when I was confronted by church denominational difficulties. Her death at sixty-two has been a great loss not only to me but also for many who knew her. I had thought of taking over where she left off, in fact I started by writing a précis

J. Edwin Warkentin

on tithing. Although I have the academic background to put something like this together, I do not have the theological credibility necessary; I found this out when I was asked to teach an adult Sunday school class in one of our Baptist churches.

I would be remiss if I did not tell you about an incident or two while I was a deacon in our church. The board of deacons divided up the church members, alphabetically, to be somewhat responsible for helping where help was needed. I had R and S. It came near Christmas time when we were each given a basket of fruit for sick, old or handicapped members. I had three baskets for three church members I had to visit, but visiting without an invitation was not—and still is not—my style, besides I did not really know those people. The fruit in my car was beginning to look ripe especially the bananas, so I had to cast diplomacy aside and get it done.

The first call was to a gentleman who lived in a CNIB housing unit. To lend a hand in this venture I asked my daughter-in-law Lois, Eric's wife, who is blind, to help me. She gladly agreed and asked if she could she take her seeing-eye dog along. Of course; this was getting easier all the time. So the next evening the three of us called on the blind gentleman. While they were discussing his hobby, which was reel to reel taping of overseas programs from his shortwave radio—evident by the discarded tapes ankle deep on the floor—the pup and I sat in the corner. Eventually I had to bring this technical discussion to a close.

Since that had gone better than I had expected, why not try the next visit? One of the ladies from our church was in the psychiatric ward of the Vancouver General Hospital, so that was our next goal. When the three of us walked in, the patients—about twelve of them—and a pianist were murdering several Christmas carols. The pianist was having a difficult time trying to get everyone to sing the same carol at the same time. The lady we came to visit spotted us; she took us to visit in a different room. The lady asked Lois about being blind: had Lois not seen her husband all these years, had she not seen the mountains or her daughter? Lois, my daughter-in-law (more like a daughter) had become used to her handicap and with her normal cheerful face and positive disposition made a deep impression on the person we had come to see; so much so that the family problems which were her reasons for being in the ward vanished, and she was back with her family by the end of the week. My visits had gone so well that we figured me might as well try the third one, which was across the road from Vancouver city hall and not far from the hospital. When I rang the doorbell, an elderly lady answered, she told us that the woman we had hoped to visit had moved, she had the address which was several miles away. As it was getting late, I said that I could handle this one myself, after all I had seen how it was done. I took Lois and Lisa, her dog, back to their home, and I went home too.

The next evening with the last basket of fruit still in my car, I set out. As it turned out I would not have been able to find that address in the dark, but I did find the lady, who was living in a care home. She was well into her eighties; she told me all about her childhood and her growing up and about most of her life. Before I left I gave her the basket of fast-decomposing fruit. She died the next day. I wondered if the shock of someone visiting her or the fruit had contributed to her death.

For three consecutive years, in the 1970s, at Convention sessions, I was elected president of the British Columbia Fellowship Baptist Churches. This was followed by a term as president of the

Canadian Fellowship Baptist Churches, headquartered in Toronto. It was rare—and still is—for a person without professional or specialized theological studies to be accepted in these offices. Many times while in meetings with the various Boards in Toronto, the members of which had holy orders confirmed on them (ordained), I was aware that I was being just tolerated; but being president, I needed to know about the plans of the various departments. It surprised me that there never seemed to be a business plan or methodology when it came to approaching most matters.

During my period in British Columbia, I was asked by the Council to look into a few Baptist churches throughout the province and bring back a report as to whether they should still be supported, especially financially, which had been the case for decades. The result was that three were closed and their resources—especially the *human* resources—were applied elsewhere; when I reported these findings at the Annual General Convention sessions several *reverends* called me to task, accusing me of being ruthless rather than merciful, in fact one of the *divines* accused me of "not knowing what a soul is worth." Another preacher told me to not rock the boat!

To not open a church work, prior to starting a mission, was better than having it closed after devout people had supported it for a length of time. One of the reverends especially, whose voice quivered with rage at my insensitivity, was my case example. He had moved to the eastern area of BC from Ottawa to start a new Baptist church. Without a business plan or a source of finances, he and his little congregation in a remote BC region, built a rather nice building. Then he left for greener pastures in Vancouver. The poor people he left behind were left with a large debt. My wife and I spent a month in the summer camping in our truck camper next to the church building. I visited everyone who was associated with the mission to give me their opinion of its future. With the information and my personal point of view, decisions were made by the Home Missions Board—and not by me although my findings likely influenced them—and the site was shut down. So often I heard the term "God called me" here or there, as it suited. My view has been—and still is—that people are called to *salvation*, but then to elaborate on the call assignment, especially from God might be rather dubious.

Let me tell you one more theological incident, and then I will go on to a more interesting phase of my life. In the early 1980s, I helped start a Baptist presence in South-East Vancouver. The city of Vancouver had just built a splendid recreation centre in the community where we and several other church-going families and single people lived. Prior to this time we had met in a school at the foot of Burnaby Mountain. Now it seemed practical that we try to be allotted space in this new building. Because I had time, I was asked to approach Vancouver City Hall to apply for space for an hour Sunday mornings. City Hall granted us space for an hour each Sunday morning. We were recognized as Champlain Heights Baptist Church. A few weeks later, the Vancouver City Manager came to see me with a problem. Two other denominations had demanded equal time and he did not know how to resolve the problem, since only one hour was available. I told him I would take it up with the membership. After a discussion one of the members suggested we call ourselves Champlain Heights Community Church. We all agreed to the name change. The city manager was greatly relieved and thanked us.

It was not long after that I was called on the carpet of the BC Baptist Fellowship Convention Executive Board, the group I had previously represented. I explained how this had come about, and then the committee told me that, if we did not reinstate Baptist in our name, we would be stricken off the BC Fellowship Baptist roll—a form of shunning—and I would not be permitted to address the Convention in session; this was the organization I had represented on the French Missions Board as well as Home Missions and various other committees, and as president. Our church was excommunicated, as it were, and my association with the Convention came to an end. Although I felt regretful that such a decision could be made without the Convention membership being consulted, I felt as though a great burden rolled off my back. I have been on sabbatical ever since.

SEVENTEEN

West Coast Beckons

Alfred, Marjorie's father, died in 1964. That and the trouble with the preacher of the church we were attending convinced Marjorie and I decided to move to Victoria, BC, not far from Patricia Bay where I had been assigned when with the air force. We had special memories of our previous residence in that part of BC.

We sold our farm and got rid of our zoo. I took a leave of absence from my job with Alberta Government Telephones, bought an old farm truck, and toward the end of August, we set out. Marjorie drove our car and pulled our camping trailer while one of the children, they took turns, and I made for Calgary where we stayed overnight at the home of one of my aunt's. We left in earnest next morning, through about three inches of snow, for the high hills that separates Alberta from British Columbia. We had travelled just into BC, when one of the truck's rear axles had broken down, actually it was a bearing that broke. The truck limped into a garage, and I had it repaired. We then proceeded, under a bright clear sky, until we were twenty-five miles from Golden, BC, when Marjorie, travelling behind us, sounded the car's horn. I looked in the rear view mirror and saw the wheel and axle were almost totally out of their housing.

I parked the truck on the road shoulder and climbed into the car heading for Golden. A tow truck went back to our truck and towed it to Golden. We had our camper trailer set up in one of the city's parks. Early next morning Louise, Judie, and I drove to Calgary to pick up a new axle—the old one was bent—and some new bearings. The mechanic at our last trouble spot had put the new bearings in backwards. After that we sailed right along until we came to the ferry that took us to Vancouver Island.

A friend of ours from former Island days had found a house for us on Monterey Road in the Oak Bay area of Victoria. We stayed at that address for two months while I looked for a house we could buy. One way or another, the former Canadian ambassador to Japan heard that we were looking for a house, the result was that we bought his house on St. Patrick Street, Oak Bay.

Prior to moving from Edmonton to Victoria, I applied and was given tentative employment with BC Telephones (BCTel) and BC Hydro on the basis of my microwave telecommunications experience; it just required that I show up for interviews. Both companies were establishing extensive microwave communication systems throughout British Columbia. Upon our family's arrival in Victoria, I visited both corporations to report my presence and to make formal interviews for employment. Neither of them impressed me with what they had lined up for me. BCTel wanted to send me up the coast to Truch Island near Prince Rupert for their microwave Scatter System. We had come to Victoria to get away from winters and isolation; I had spent two terms in Northern isolation sites with the air force, which I thought was my quota. BC Hydro on the other hand wanted me to develop a maintenance schedule for their microwave sites, again something with which I had extensive experience. When

I asked what was in store for me after I had finished, their response was too evasive for me to plan a career; maybe this or maybe that.

A friend of mine in Edmonton suggested I get into life insurance sales as he had done very successfully. I wrote the tests in Vancouver, for a well-known insurance agency, the same one with which my Edmonton friend was employed. The company teamed me up with an insurance agent in Victoria, who was also in the provincial government cabinet. He suggested I join a church and a couple of social associations to cultivate these organizations for clients. To join anything in order to take advantage of new-found friends was not in my plans, so employment with either corporation never materialized. What was I to do now?

In desperation, I applied for a job with Alberta Government Telephones, my previous employer in Edmonton. They offered to take me back with a significant pay raise with the title of Systems Engineer. With a feeling of extreme anxiety, I bid my family adieu on Boxing Day 1965 and went to Edmonton.

We had kept the house Marjorie's parents had built—I had bought it from her father's estate. Our plan now was to move back to Edmonton and live happily ever after. The job at AGT turned out to be in the area I had only dreamed about, which was designing microwave routes for new radio systems in the near future. These were to be in the mountainous areas of Alberta, including over a few lakes. In the meantime Marjorie was scanning the Victoria papers every day for a job posting for which I might apply. I had told her that anything would be worthwhile so that we might remain in Victoria. She spotted two positions. This was January 1966, and I was forty-two years old. One job was as a postman, and the other was with the Canadian navy as a journeyman electronics technician.

I was given time off from my job to temporarily return to Victoria. I wrote the postal exam along with about forty other candidates, and then I had my interview with the federal civil service for the navy job. I was successful in both tests, but I thought the navy job would be more challenging and might develop into a career so I took it—starting in a month. Returning to Edmonton I explained that my children had settled down in school and another move might be detrimental to their schooling, among other reasons to stay in Victoria. The engineering department personnel understood, letting me resign for the second time in six months.

I applied as an engineering assistant with the Canadian navy. The Canadian navy along with the American navy were testing new anti-submarine torpedoes. The testing area was in the deep channel of Georgia Straight just off Parksville on Vancouver Island. My position was a union position. After studying the literature and the sequence of firing and retrieving the prototype units it came to me that con-siderable time and money could be saved if certain modifications would be made. The union shop steward told me that he could have me fired for reaching into areas reserved for professional engineers. The engineers studied what I presented to them and made some of the modifications. I did not remain with the navy much longer. This happened once more, so I looked for an escape exit.

I was a journeyman electrical/electronics technician, so I made application with the University of Victoria (UVic) to take the aca-demic program for teaching shop courses to high school students. At a social meeting, I met a man who was the shop teacher at a Vancouver Island high school. Upon asking him how to proceed with an application for such a position, as he had done two years earlier, he told me that he had responded to a newspaper advertisement placed there by the Ministry of Education. He was a journeyman carpenter—with four academic courses, which he had taken during summer school, he was given the teaching position. This possibility appealed to me as the escape channel for which I had been seeking. UVic accepted me as a student. giving me full credits for my courses at the University of Manitoba, twenty years earlier. During this time I noticed an advertisement in one of the local newspapers; British Columbia Institute of Technology (BCIT) in Burnaby was looking for an instructor to teach courses in microwave telecommunications technology, starting in July 1967. The better offer came from BCIT, which I accepted after I had been interviewed by the Electrical Department dean and one of his chief instructors. The salary was twice what I had been receiving from the navy. It was the first week of July, and since classes did not start until September, I was given five weeks leave with pay. I needed that to find room and board near the campus, buy a car and do some chores around our house in Victoria. Once the courses started in September 1967, I commuted home to Victoria every weekend for a year. This was to make certain that I wished to continue with my new-found work and to consider the good for our children; it proved the best for all concerned. There were two occasions during the year when I told the dean that I would not return on Monday. He said I would be back, and so I was. Several of my teaching colleagues questioned my technical background, asking for my academic qualifications; of course I had none, but in time, perhaps ten years later, through hard work and sacrifice, I had acquired more education qualifying university degrees than my former detractors. In fact, I became their department head, Associate Dean of Electrical Engineering. During my first year at BCIT, my main responsibilities were to develop a course teaching new students the components of electronic equipment and circuits—their compositions and characteristics in electronic circuits. In time I was asked to develop two courses which the students would be taking in their graduation year. One of the courses was Sound System Engineering, a course that was not taught anywhere in Canada, yet was very necessary for effective transmission of voice and music, especially in theatres, music and lecture locations, churches, and sporting facilities. The other course was Microwave Telecommunications Systems, this one was right up my alley since I had several years experience in designing, installing, and maintaining a number of systems in previous years. For this course, I understudied the very bright instructor who designed the microwave curriculum, by sitting in his lectures and helping with the lab work. He was the professional academic teacher, and I was the experienced technologist. He went on to develop and teach courses in micro-electronics and robotics, and I took over microwave systems.

The time came, soon after I started teaching, that I realized my post-secondary education was lacking. To register for an engineering degree would take four years as a full-time student, which was financially not feasible so I looked to other avenues. In order to keep myself up to date, I enrolled first in UBC studies in an Adult Education program developing courses for teaching adults, the equivalent to a bachelor's degree. Upon completion of the program, the need for more education became apparent. I registered in a graduate program of studies in education administration at Simon Fraser University, which led to a Master of Arts (Education Administration) degree. Both of these programs were taken at night school and summer sessions for eight years. The latter degree provided me with the qualifications to become the Associate Dean of the British Columbia

Institute of Technology's Electrical Engineering Department upon the retirement of the incumbent. This position permitted me to bring about several changes in the department's program: Co-op Education, which permitted students to take up two three-month positions in industries prior to graduation. These well-paid work sessions became very popular, not only for the students but also for potential employers. The students were given a list of available co-op industry associates from which to choose. This gave the students and their employers an opportunity to make decisions prior to the students' graduation. Another well-thought-out part of education was to employ Computer Aided Instructions (CAI). The courses were modularized; the student was able to travel at his/her own speed by responding to the questions generated on the computers by the full-time instructors. A "pass" of each module required a mark of 90% or better for the tests which followed each module. It was necessary for the student, given two tries, to reach that mark before he/she could proceed to the next module. These tests were built into the module by the instructors responsible for those courses.

I travelled to the Massachusetts Institute of Technology (MIT) to learn how they had incorporated CAI in their study courses. MIT's faculty members were exceptionally helpful; many of their practices became integral parts of BCIT's electrical engineering programs. Upon my return, the instructors were offered one thousand dollars to modularize each of the courses which they had been teaching.

Perhaps the most far-reaching change I brought about was to move away from the single admission, single graduation per year. For several years I had been troubled that our laboratories were idle for three months in the summer every year. The equipment, which had cost millions of dollars, lay idle for that period. What

J. Edwin Warkentin

happened was the Electrical Department changed to several entries and several graduations each year. The president of the school along with the vice-president of education and the registrar authorized the changes—all three new programs. The thought behind these changes was that, if the largest department, the Electrical Engineering Department, could make it work, then the system could gradually be worked into the other schools on campus.

After I had been the associate dean of Engineering for several years, I was offered the opportunity to head up the Aviation and Aerospace Department located at the Vancouver International Airport. This was to be my final and perhaps the most enjoyable position I had at the Institute. Several instructors were pilots with a commendable work ethic, which they demanded of their students. Although the mechanics were dealing with oils and grease, the work benches and floors were kept spotlessly clean, which impressed not only me but also periodic inspectors from the aircraft industries. I had worked at the school for twenty-one years. At sixty-three years of age, I took early retirement to pursue other interests.

When Marjorie died from a massive heart attack in 1984, she was sixty-two, and we had been married for forty years. We'd had seven children together, and had been blessed with a healthy crop of grandchildren, and great-grandchildren. I was distraught. She and I had, in a way, grown up together—maybe more so for me. In order to spend personal time trying to deal with my grief, I went to work at seven o'clock in the morning and returned home at eight o'clock in the evening.

In 1983 a Japanese university professor, Akiyama, and ten of his engineering students from a university in Kyoto, Japan visited BCIT to learn how topics similar to theirs were taught. I had spent much time showing him around BCIT's Burnaby campus and discussing the electrical engineering curricula; upon leaving he gave me his business card, which I promptly put it in a dresser drawer and forgot. To assist me in my time of grief, my brother Peter, who had retired from a military career as a captain, suggested that he and I go to Japan. That seemed like a good idea. Though it was a place where I did not know anyone—or the language for that matter—I felt that it might give me time to think things over. Then I remembered the business card that Akiyama had given me. I sent him a telegram, stating when and where we would be in Tokyo.

Peter and I flew to Hong Kong by Korean Airways via Los Angeles and Seoul. While in Hong Kong, we took a side trip to mainland China. The poverty of that part of China was evident. The stores had very few items on their shelves, very few cars were evident and those that were visible were associated with government agencies. Peter and I had suits made for us within twenty-four hours. It amazed me that many Chinese in Hong Kong lived on boats, very few of these had engines; it was like an urban subdivision. After staying in Hong Kong for a few days, we travelled to Tokyo, where we met professor Akiyama. He suggested we stop off in Japan's ancient capital of Nara when we travelled to Kyoto. He had two of his staff waiting for us when we arrived, and they showed us through the city. To get on the train to Kyoto, we had to make reservations. We almost missed our train; in fact, just as we stepped on the train, the well-known Bullet Train, it left the station.

Professor Akiyama came and showed us through his Alma Mater, the University of Tokyo. He had been a fighter pilot for Japan's air force during their Pacific war. Before leaving us in Tokyo, he invited us to his home in Kyoto. We did that about a week later, travelling

J. Edwin Warkentin

by the Bullet Train. In the meantime, Peter and I travelled by trains to various rural areas, feeling perfectly safe at all times. We also took part in several Japanese functions, such as Flower Arranging, visiting the Emperor's gardens and park, and marvelling at the cleanliness of the city.

When we visited with the professor in Kyoto, he showed us through a local factory operated by robots. The factory made and assembled electric motors. A staff of two or three people supplied the robots with parts for the motors, making sure that each one had enough components until the following morning. These employees made certain that the mechanical parts of the robots were in good order. We had dinner with the professor and his wife at their home in Kyoto. It was a delightful evening, except for the table which was only 18 inches off the floor. The idea was, I assumed, to get to the table in time to put your legs under the table first. Peter beat me to it, so I did a lot of shifting around to keep the blood circulating.

It was soon time to return to our way of living although we did spend a bit of time in Taiwan and in Hawaii, which in itself was worth the trip. I had made up my mind to ask Patricia Doidge to marry me. Pat had known Marjorie and our children. She was employed in the chemistry department of Simon Fraser University, processing professors' dissertations and research reports. She had not been married. I was surprised, as were her relatives and friends, that she accepted my proposal. If I was to marry again, I wanted someone who had no children, I had enough for the two of us, and I also wanted someone who would not bring along much baggage. She made no demands but rather encouraged me in my decision to take early retirement and get into picture framing. In fact, as I got into teaching picture framing to classes of students, she was the one-on-one person to help individual students with their assignments. She also managed all the business and financial aspects of our operation.

EIGHTEEN

Retirement Again

Upon Patricia's and my retirements we—more like I—decided to leave my past working milieu, especially my electronics life; they had been challenging and enjoyable for several decades.

In my last year at the British Columbia Institute of Technology, I was given the responsibility of heading up the Institute's aerospace programs, which included aircraft maintenance. Things were being done much like they always had been with regard to the instruction syllabi. Computers were coming into their own for teaching courses. Co-operative education had been implemented in the universities. There was a serious demand for operational aircraft for practical experience. The provincial government provided the school with a large, modern hangar from an airline that had merged with another airline. These were events in which I played a major part by meeting with Premier Bill Vander Zalm to go over the transfer of the hangar.

During my first year of retirement, I with the manager of a private airline combined to form a school of aircraft maintenance. The programs at BCIT had long waiting entry lists, some as long as two years. We had space in one of the older hangars at the Vancouver International Airport. As it turned out, the first graduating class of six students would be our last class because the manager of the private airline died in a plane crash; he had been our funding and publicity source. What to do now?

One evening in 1986, while Patricia was scanning through the local paper, she spotted an advertisement offering a night school course in picture framing. We had discussed what we would like to do, and picture framing had come up. It was a six-evening presentation, so we enrolled. The course was not presented very well; we were a class of twenty-seven and the professor had only enough equipment for one person. Pat and I would usually go home halfway through the evening—at coffee time—since we had not touched any of the projects, and I for one had lost interest. The class had dwindled down from twenty-seven to twelve. However, it was the first time I had ever seen what might be involved in a real picture framing business, so the prospect for this line of work became appealing. I could see the possibility of a picture framing/art gallery business. Since there was not a picture framing school in Canada, we both travelled to various American centres where classes were being given. After several weeks looking in catalogues for equipment ideas and studying existing picture galleries for suggestions, we rented a building in New Westminster, BC, which in my research appeared to have very little in the way of picture framing businesses. I had not retired, neither had Pat, so my brother Peter who had retired from a military career agreed to attend a picture framing school in California for a week. He then took over the business, letting Pat and I run it on Friday evenings and Saturdays. The learning curve went nearly straight up. I took a course in small business management at night school. We bought $20,000 worth of equipment and supplies to start up. I enjoyed operating a small business, but to have it involving picture framing and art became even more attractive. It took us a while to understand the various levels of art and their monetary value. There were prints made off artists' original paintings; how well the artist was known would often determined the values of the prints. Before long, I saw the need for a picture framing school in Canada. While Pat and I were still working for salaries—and not very confident in our framing skills—I hired five competent individuals; one a day with their particular proficiency for the day they would be there. I set the curriculum which resulted, in part, from the results of a survey of frame shops in the Vancouver and lower mainland area.

Monday—An introduction and familiarization with the equipment. The organization of a shop and safety standards. Cutting mat board. Finding out what the students' objectives were.

Tuesday—Mat board design; cutting square, rectangle, oval and circle openings with specific assignments.

Wednesday—Colour coordination, glass cutting, needle work mounting, and canvas painting handling and stretching; ready for framing.

Thursday—Frame cutting day, when the learners would practice cutting wood and metal mouldings keeping safety in mind and then assemble a project started earlier in the week and frame it completely with a metal frame, along with a project with a wood frame.

Friday—Business day, controlling inventory, promotion and advertising, pricing and a list of picture framing supply sources followed by a written and a practical test. The participants would then be required to frame their certificates. We had students from all over Canada, the United States as well as from other countries.

It seemed to me that an ideal setting for a school might be in a working picture framing shop. We tried that for a few months, but the frame shop customers started interfering with our *fun* classes, so we sold the shop and concentrated on the school. We started another school in the Toronto area (Markham to be specific). Our schedule at that point was one week in the Vancouver area, relax for a week, then off to Markham, then relax for another week. After six years of schooling, we sold the schools and published a magazine intended for the picture framing industry. That lasted for three years, after which we could not subsidize it any longer. As an aside, while mulling over the magazine venture, I had a session with a publishing professor from a local university. He gave me some publications and some valuable advice. When he left me he cautioned, "Unless you have $200,000 in your pocket to spend on something about which you do not have a clue, you would be smart to forget the whole idea." When the magazine folded, I was almost $200,000 in debt, which was paid off in four years at the cost of completely paying for our house.

Patricia and I developed a shortened picture framing course, taking it up-country to the regional colleges throughout the province and into Saskatchewan. This period was likely the most enjoyable of our after-retirement activities. We met some very interesting people and saw many attractive parts of the country, which otherwise we never would have seen. Then Patricia became ill with Multiple Sclerosis, so we retired once again. She could not stand up any more, and I would not—indeed could not—do the work by myself, so regrettably we retired once more. Since retiring I have written and published a book—*Picture Framing as a Business.*

Years have passed, so Patricia and I have located a seniors' residence that provides all the present necessities and also has provisions for future care, medical and physical, should this become necessary. Patricia, who came down with multiple sclerosis in her late 50s, is in the extended care unit of this residence. Since we live but one storey from each other in the same building, I see her every day. I spend most of my time retiring and working on my computer. As I become more adept with the computer, perhaps I might even consider writing some short articles. In the meantime, I find it easier to keep in touch with relatives and other friends via the internet.

Edwin Warkentin

Edwin Warkentin enlisted in the Royal Canadian Air Force during World War II as a wireless operator when he was eighteen, serving both in Canada and overseas. After the war he attended University of Manitoba for two years. Afterward he went back into the RCAF for ten years, stationed much of his time in Northern Canada. While with the military he studied electrical engineering which enabled him to take a position as assistant engineer with a telecom corporation in Alberta.

For fifteen years, he held a faculty position with the British Columbia Institute of Technology teaching Microwave Engineering Systems and developing a Sound Systems Engineering program. By taking night school and summer semester programs for eight years he graduated with his Master of Arts (Education) degree which was followed by his appointment as the Associate Dean of Electrical Engineering at BCIT. Edwin lives with his wife, Patricia, in Langley, B.C.

CPSIA information can be obtained at www.ICGtesting.com
Printed in the USA
LVOW06s0348020813

345854LV00001B/52/P